SELF-ACTUALIZATION

GARLAND REFERENCE LIBRARY
OF SOCIAL SCIENCE
(VOL. 352)

SELF-ACTUALIZATION
An Annotated Bibliography of Theory and Research

I. David Welch

George A. Tate

Donald C. Medeiros

GARLAND PUBLISHING, INC. • NEW YORK & LONDON
1987

Library of Congress Cataloging-in-Publication Data

Welch, I. David, 1940–
Self-actualization.

(Garland reference library of social science ;
vol. 352)
Includes indexes.
1. Self-actualization (Psychology)—Bibliography.
I. Tate, George A.   II. Medeiros, Donald C.
III. Title.   IV. Series: Garland reference library
of social science ; v. 352.
Z7204.S42W44   1987   [BF637.S4]   016.1552   86-31996
ISBN 0-8240-8568-X (alk. paper)

Printed on acid-free, 250-year-life paper
Manufactured in the United States of America

CONTENTS

CONTENTS

ACKNOWLEDGEMENTS

We wish to express our appreciation to the faculty and staff of the James A. Michener Library of the University of Northern Colorado without whose assistance this work could not have been completed. We especially wish to thank the staff of the library who work in the areas of computer assisted reference searches, inter-library loan, reference, periodicals and circulation.

Also, the editors wish to thank Mr. Guy Roberts for his assistance in helping the editors fight our way through the complexities of word processing.

Dr. Daniel Bruns proofread the manuscript and, for this tiresome and necessary task, we sincerely thank him.

Ms. Edith Israel prepared the subject index for this volume. This important job she did thoroughly and well. We appreciate her work and are confident the readers will as well since her work makes locating subjects and topics much easier.

Additionally, to the editors of Garland Publishing, who consented to the work and provided help throughout, we extend our thanks.

Finally, the editors appreciate the assistance of the Scholarly Assistance Funds of the Graduate School and the College of Education of the University of Northern Colorado whose financial support made the extensive computer searches of literature possible and without which this project would likely not have been completed.

INTRODUCTION

Self-actualization as a concept is a relatively modern idea. The person most associated with the concept is undoubtedly Abraham Maslow. While Maslow did not originate the term, he did more to popularize it than any other single individual. The concept of actualization is important because it stands in opposition to another major theory of mental health - adjustment. Adjustment theory is the major approach of the Freudian or Psychoanalytic and Behavioral orientations in psychology. The introduction of the concept of actualization can be credited with at least 4 major accomplishment. First, it challenged the concept of adjustment to a society or culture as the major factor in establishing psychological health. Second, it provided a way out of the problem of cultural relativism and sought to provide a description of psychological health that was universal and transcended both cultural and time. Third, it presented a new image of human beings as more than driven by constant intra-psychic warfare or determined entirely by environmental conditions. Finally, it provided the basis for the development of a third force in psychology - humanistic psychology. In spite of these contributions, the study of self-actualization, indeed the focus on positive psychological development as opposed to negative psychological development, remains a minority concern in the mainstream of modern psychological thought. Witness the total number of references in this book, which represents a thorough, if not complete, listing of the references in the English language. This total would hardly scratch the surface of writings concerned with pathology. Nevertheless, it is a major concern of psychology and one which has implications far outside the domain of psychology alone as the sources in this volume testify.

The purpose of this document

The purpose of this volume is to provide the

reader with a ready reference to the major works dealing with self-actualization. It has been the editors' intention to collect into a single volume all of the writings in the English language concerning self-actualization. It will be obvious to anyone who engages in such an endeavor that we have not actualized our goal. We do believe, however, that we have collected here a clear majority of the writings on self-actualization. Given that we started with an unknown, there is no real way to determine how much of the total we have collected. We are confident that most writings are included in this work. This collection will become increasing complete with the help of the reader. We have provided a reference form at the end of the book where the reader may send any work not included in this volume that should be included. We will revise this work from time-to-time not only to update it but to include works left out of this first edition.

We approached this collection by having a computer search done of such key words as: self-actualization, fully functioning self, adequate personality, productive personality, mature personality, personality integration , self-fulfillment and self-realization. We did not use the term mental health since so much that is published under that title concerns not the healthy personality but the disorganized one that it did not seem beneficial or appropriate. After the computer assisted search, we collected those works and used the bibliography in each reference to cross check to make sure we had captured all of the sources. We, of course, had not and we went through approximately 7 major searches before we began to find no additional sources in any new reference we found. Finally, we reached a place where in the computer searches (3) and the manual searches (7) we found no sources that we did not already have. It is our conviction that we have located and referenced the major, and perhaps most, of the sources concerned with self-actualization in the English language. The one exception to this could be master's level theses which we were unable to track except through article bibliographies.

We have arbitrarily divided this book into

sections. The sections separate self-actualization
theory, research and practice into categories that
made sense to the editors. Naturally, other
categories could have replaced those but it was for
convenience that we separated them as we have. If
this organization does not prove helpful, there are
2 indices to aid the reader. First, there is an
author index. Second, there is a subject index
that includes topics mentioned in the titles of the
referenced material. It is our hope that such a
quick way of finding particular subjects or
concerns will be of assistance to the student,
researcher and/or writer using this book. The
major sections in this work are: aging,
creativity, criticisms, death and dying, education,
intimacy, love, marriage and the family,
instruments, management, meditation, minorities,
pathology, peak experiences, psychotherapy,
religion, sex, sports, theory, values and women.
Each of these sections provides the complete
reference and a short annotation for article
particular to that section. In addition, a
reference is provided for dissertations and theses
dealing with the specific topic of the section.
Finally, a section of books is provided with a
complete reference for each book listed. Both an
Author Index and a Subject Index are included as
further aids for quickly finding a particular
author and topic.

Who will use this book

Obviously, this is not a book for the general
public. It is intended for serious students of a
particular concept in psychological theory.
Students who are interested in a quick overview of
the concept of self-actualization will profit from
it; researchers who need to know previous research
in a topic area will find it useful; scholars who
wish to include the concept of self-actualization
in other sources will have a ready reference for
their summations; and, honors, master's and
doctoral level students considering self-
actualization as a topic for research will find in
these pages areas badly in need of further
research. It is for these reasons that this volume
has been assembled.

Self-Actualization

SELF ACTUALIZATION:
AN ANNOTATED BIBLIOGRAPHY OF THEORY AND RESEARCH

Aging

The potential for self-actualization in later
adulthood, coupled with what appears to be a
dearth of studies and research in this area,
gives an indication of a need for further
study. It is unclear whether the editors of
this volume have simply overlooked some source
of writings in this area or whether, in fact,
so little has been written. If we have
overlooked sources, we appeal to the reader to
send us those at the address included at the
end of this book. In any case, there appears
to be a need for studies of aging and self-
actualization that might include: (a) self-
image and life-satisfaction, (b) role and
function of empathy and/or support systems, (c)
locus-of-control and impact of internal and
external stresses and (d) of self-report
studies investigating the personal perceptions
of psychologically healthy older adults
concerning what they have to teach those
younger than themselves.

1. Box, T. A. & Peck, D. L. (1981, December).
    Perceived low self-actualization and external
    fatalistic determinism as a function of aging.
    Journal of Genetic Psychology, 139(2), 295-304.

    Reports the results of research which tested
    for perceived differences in locus of control
    in an aging population. The results suggest a
    difference in self-actualization and social
    control was apparent in two groups tested.

2. Keahey, S. P. & Seaman, D. F. (1974, Spring).
    Self-actualization and adjustment in
    retirement: Implications for program
    development. Adult Education, 24(3), 220-226.

1

Investigated the relationship of concepts of self-actualization to successful retirement. The results show that a measure of self-actualization and a measure of successful retirement were correlated and significant. The authors conclude that self-actualizing concepts are involved in successful retirement.

Dissertations and Theses (Note: Throughout this book Dissertation Abstracts International will be abbreviated DAI.)

3. Cuje, B. B. (1984). An investigation of the effects of human potential seminars on the self-actualization of older adults (ages 60-85). DAI, 45(8), 2447A.

4. Eargle, D. I. (1980). Reminiscence and self-actualization: Relationship to residential setting of elderly. DAI, 41(6), 2383B.

5. Flynn, R. J. (1985). The relationship of self-actualization, internal locus of control, and sexual activity to the experience of life satisfaction in elderly men. DAI, 46(8), 2621B.

6. Hummel, J. F. (1985). Related factors in self-actualization and susceptibility to nutrition quackery among adult women 65 years of age and older. DAI, 46(6), 1875B.

7. Lantz, J. M. (1981). Self-actualization: An indicator of self-care practices among adults 65 years and older. DAI, 42(10), 4017B.

8. Meyer, S. L. (1975). A study of the effects of a pre-retirement workshop on the measured level of self-actualization of university civil service employees. DAI, 35(7), 4163A.

9. Moyer, L. M. (1981). The effects of empathy training on levels of self-actualization in senior citizens. DAI, 42(2), 554A.

Self-Actualization

10. Rak, G. R. (1978). Impact of age-segregated public housing upon self-actualization and other personal-adjustment variables among the aged: A ten month follow-up. <u>DAI</u>, <u>38</u>(11), 5547B.

11. Taylor, G. A. (1984). A construct validity study of life satisfaction, self-actualization, and locus of control. <u>DAI</u>, <u>45</u>(11), 3658B.

12. Tekavec, C. M. R. (1982). Self-actualization, reminiscence and life satisfaction in retired and employed older adults. <u>DAI</u>, <u>43</u>(8), 2719B.

13. Tomalty, R. L. (1985). Human potential seminars for senior adults in a community college setting: An assessment of growth in self-actualization. <u>DAI</u>, <u>46</u>(7), 1840A.

Creativity has long been identified as one of the dimensions of self-actualization. However, research into the correlation between self-actualization and creativity provides only a slight relationship. Research aimed at the clarification of the relationship between creativity and self-actualization can provide an important contribution to the field. It remains to be determined whether "conventional" ideas of creativity or some other more intra-, inter- or metapersonal form of creativity actually contributes to self-actualization.

14. Kirton, M. & Hammond, S. (1980, June). Levels of self-actualization of adaptors and innovators. Psychological Reports, 46(3, Pt. 2), 1321-1322.

Adaptors are defined as persons who tend to operate within consensually agreed paradigms. Innovators are persons who tends not to be bound by paradigms. The authors suggest "an outcome of these differences is that adaptors might be supposed to be more willing to adhere to accepted modes of thought and behavior that will mould their image of themselves and so are capable of higher self-actualization; the converse might be true of innovators." The results were unexpected in that both Adaptors and Innovators have low self-actualization scores.

15. Landau, E. & Maoz, B. (1978, January). Creativity and self-actualization in the aging personality. American Journal of Psychotherapy, 32(1), 117-127.

Investigated the relationship between coping with aging, death anxiety and levels of self-actualization. The results showed that the higher self-actualizing scores and creativity

4

scores, the better the persons coped with aging and exhibited less denial of death.

16. Maslow, A. H. (1965). The need for creative people. _Personnel Administration_, _28_, 3-5, 21-22.

Outlines some of the importance of the need for creative people and the increasing need for them in society. Presents some differences between science and creativity and the types of persons needed in each enterprise. Argues that the need in society is not for "product" creativity so much as it is to help persons develop in the "process" stages of creativity.

17. Maslow, A. H. (1963). The creative attitude. _The Structurist_, _3_, 4-10.

Presents a discussion that the concept of creativity and the concept of self-actualization seem highly similar and may turn out to be the same concept. The second half of the article outlines characteristics of the peak experience and how similar these are to the creative moment/attitude.

18. Maslow, A. H. (1959). Creativity in self-actualizing people. In H. H. Anderson (Ed.) _Creativity and its cultivation_ (1959). New York: Harpers and Row.

Provides the author's changing views of creativity as a result of his investigation into the characteristics of self-actualizing people. Maslow describes a difference between "special talent creativeness" from "self-actualizing creativeness." Also, included in this chapter is a discussion of the place of the peak experience in creativity.

19. Maslow, A. H. (1949). The expressive component of behavior. _Psychological Review_, _56_, 261-272.

Expressive behavior is considered to be non-instrumental or not directed to a particular point. Coping behavior is functional, purposive or instrumental. This article explores the differences between the two types of behavior. Expressive behavior is explored as "the beauty of a beautiful woman, the slumping posture, lowered tonus, and hopeless expression of the depressed person, the style of handwriting, walking, smiling, dancing, etc. These are non-purposive. They have no aim and no goal. They were not elaborated for the sake of need gratification."

20. Mathes, E. W. (1978, August). Self-actualization, metavalues, and creativity. Psychological Reports, 43(1), 215-222.

Study attempted a replication of Maslow's informal study of self-actualizing people and metavalues. The study correlated scores on a measure of self-actualization with endorsement of metavalues and measures of creativity. The results confirmed Maslow's suggestions of a relationship between self-actualization and metavalues but showed no relationship of self-actualization to creativity.

21. Murphy, J. P., Dauw, D. C., Horton, R. E., & Fredian, A. J. (1976) Self-actualization and creativity. Journal of Creative Behavior, 10(1), 39-44.

Study attempted to investigate similarities and differences between concepts of self-actualization and creativity. Two measures of self-actualization and two measures of creativity were used with 177 graduate and undergraduate students. The results showed some clear-cut statistical results while other relationships were less clear. The measures of creativity were highly related to one another as were the two measures of self-actualization. However, creativity and self-actualization revealed no strong relationship.

22. Regelski, T. A. (1973, Fall). Self-actualization in creating and responding to art. Journal of Humanistic Psychology, 13(4), 57-68.

6

Presents a case that the arts provide a limitless source of peak experiences and thus can be used as a foundation for personal growth. Argues that the arts are neither "fun and games" nor high culture but rather represent a fundamental human need. However, suggests that if this is the case the presentation of the arts to students must be altered.

23. Walton, D. R. (1973, November). Effects of personal growth groups on self-actualization and creative personality. Journal of College Student Personnel, 14(6), 490-494.

    Reports a study in which some students were taught concepts of self-actualization and others were given experiential training designed to promote self-actualization. The results were that the experiential groups promoted higher self-actualization and creative health than the directly taught groups.

24. Yonge, G. D. (1975, December). Time experiences, self-actualizing values, and creativity. Journal of Personality Assessment, 39(6), 601-606.

    Investigated the relationship between certain experiences of time, self-actualization and creativity. The results show a confluence between these various concepts and provides some evidence for the validity of the instruments used.

Dissertations and Theses

25. Cozzi, E. A. (1977). Self-actualization in selected plays of Ugo Betti. DAI, 38(10), 5799A.

26. Foley, P. M. (1977). Creativity in children as it relates to self-actualization in their parents. DAI, 39(10), 5042B.

27. Ford, S. F. S. (1979). The effects of self-awareness training on creativity and self-actualization in student teachers. <u>DAI</u>, <u>40</u>(12), 6129A.

28. James, M. H. (1985). The relationship among creativity, self-actualization, and effectiveness in teaching in selected groups of prospective teachers. <u>DAI</u>, <u>46</u>(7), 1907A.

29. Justeson, J. I. (1979). A comparison of a measure of self-actualization in selected artists and non-artists. <u>DAI</u>, <u>41</u>(1), 151A.

30. Koenig, H. F. (1973). Creativity and the fully functioning person: A test of a proposition from Rogers' theory. <u>DAI</u>, <u>34</u>(12), 6195B.

31. Malkin, S. G. (1982). A study of the interrelationships among self-actualization, creativity and openness to experience. <u>DAI</u>, <u>43</u>(4), 1238B.

32. Maul, T. L. (1970) An investigation of the relationships between self-actualization and creative thinking processes. <u>DAI</u>, <u>32</u>(2), 793A.

33. Ryder, W. W. (1985). Achieving self-actualization through art experience: A guide for instructors of elementary education students (Volumes I and II). <u>DAI</u>, <u>46</u>(8), 2167A.

34. Summerfield, L. H. (1974). The relationship of age, creativity and risk-taking to self-actualization. <u>DAI</u>, <u>35</u>(2), 1030B.

35. Tuttle, M. C. (1973). An exploration of C. G. Jung's psychological types as predictors of creativity and self-actualization. <u>DAI</u>, <u>35</u>(8), 4154B.

While a theory attempts to symbolize reality, it also distorts it to one degree or another. It seems important, therefore, that any theoretical orientation welcome criticisms from both within and outside the orientation. Self-actualization theorists have communicated such an openness to criticism some of which has produced changes in thinking that is important. Still, this remains an area which could benefit from more thinking and writing.

36. Aron, A. (1977, Spring). Maslow's other child. Journal of Humanistic Psychology, 17(2), 9-24.

Criticizes the concept of self-actualization using the hippie movement of the 1960's as an example of self-indulgence that the author sees as a synonym for self-actualization. The article suggests that Maslow ignored or underplayed the importance of ethics and politics. See Hampden-Turner (42) for a response.

37. Buss, A. R. (1979, Summer). Humanistic psychology as liberal ideology: The socio-historical roots of Maslow's theory of self-actualization. Journal of Humanistic Psychology, 19(3), 43-55.

Suggests that humanistic self-actualization theory was conceived of in reaction to the conservatism of behaviorism and psycholanalysis. The author argues that self-actualization reflects an elitist judgment of values, those of the minority decision makers. This "democratic elitism" prevents wide-spread self-actualization and, the author states, makes the theory contradictory.

38. Frankl, V. (1966, Fall). Self-transcendence as a human phenomenon. Journal of Humanistic Psychology, 6(2), 97-106.

Author proposes two specifically human phenomena that characterize human existence. First, there is self-detachment. Second, there is self-transcendence. The article argues that self-transcendence is the essence of existence and that motivational theorists who ignore self-transcendence fail to present a true picture of actual human striving. See (43) for a response.

39. Geller, L. (1984, Spring). Another look at self-actualization. Journal of Humanistic Psychology, 24(2), 93-106.

Debates that if the need hierarchy of Maslow is determined partially by the environment, then it no longer applies to all humans due to socio-cultural differences. The author argues that the Self is not pre-existing and the self-actualization process doesn't apply to all persons. See also (40) and (41).

40. Geller, L. (1982, Spring). The failure of self-actualization theory: A critique of Carl Rogers and Abraham Maslow. Journal of Humanistic Psychology, 22(2), 56-73.

A complex, technical and severe criticism of self-actualization theory. The author believes that the theory is atomistic and does not adequately address a person's interaction with society. The author attempts to demonstrate that the theoretical assumptions of both Carl Rogers and Abraham Maslow are incorrect. The article argues that self-actualization supports dehumanization. See also (39) and (41).

41. Ginsberg, C. (1984, Spring). Toward a somatic understanding of self: A reply to Leonard Geller. Journal of Humanistic Psychology, 24(2), 66-92.

Criticizes Geller (40) and establishes a basis for understanding the Self as both biological and environmental which is not fixed, but always in process through feedback mechanisms. Individuals may become alienated but the theory and practice of self-actualization theory attempts to diminish this. See also (39) for a response.

42. Hampden-Turner, C. (1977, Spring). Comment on "Maslow's other child." Journal of Humanistic Psychology, 17(2), 25-31.

A response to Aron (36) in which the author suggests that the criticisms made by Aron are based in part upon attributing causes of events to Maslow that occurred before he had written and in major part to misunderstanding Maslow.

43. Maslow, A. H. (1966, Fall). Comments on Dr. Frankl's paper. Journal of Humanistic Psychology, 6(2), 107-112.

Agrees with much of what is presented by Frankl (38) suggesting that differences are important and that one area of disagreement is in how to advance knowledge. The author is hopeful that the theoretical discussion provoked by Frankl's article will help define "self-transcendence" and open up research.

44. Maslow, A. H. (1959). Critique of self-actualization: I. Some dangers of being-cognition. Journal of Individual Psychology, 15, 24-32.

Intended as part one of a series critiquing self-actualization. This first paper presents some dangers of the concept of B-cognition (B=being) which is in contrast to D-Cognition (D=deficiency-need-motivation) or human-centered or self-centered motivation. Maslow list 8 major dangers of B-cognition which he acknowledges as admittedly theoretical rather than practical concerns.

45. Smith, B. (1973, Spring). On self-actualization: A transambivalent examination of a focal theme in Maslow's psychology. Journal of Humanistic Psychology, 13(2), 17-33.

Self-Actualization

Criticizes Maslow's theory of self-actualization as being too one-sidedly positive in considering human nature and not taking into account historical, environmental forces leading to ethics and politics which the author sees Maslow as largely ignoring. Argues that any concept of "mental health" must be complex in order to explain human functioning.

In the encounter with death, it appears, from some studies, that the person who is more self-actualizing is better able to make that encounter less fearful and a more positive part of life. This seems to be true with regard to the way in which one perceives death, the way in which one communicates with others about death, and the manner in which one moves through the process of dying. However, other studies seem to contradict such conclusions giving a clear need for more research and study in this important aspect of self-actualization.

46. Gamble, J. W. & Brown, E. C. (1980-1981). Self-actualization and personal mortality. Omega, 11(4), 341-353.

Compared actualizing helping professionals with institutionalized patients in a state mental facility on personal ability to face death. The results indicate that "the ability to face death is a concomitant of actualized authentic existence."

47. Lester, D. & Colvin, L. M. (1977, October). Fear of death, alienation and self-actualization. Psychological Reports, 41(2), 526.

Reports that those who fear death tend to have higher scores on a measure of alienation. The study also reports that the more self-actualizing persons are the less they tend to fear death.

48. Pollak, J. M. (1978, June). Relationships between psychoanalytic personality pattern, death anxiety, and self-actualization. Perceptual and Motor Skills, 46(3, Pt 1), 846.

Study explored the relationships between psychoanalytic personality pattern such as oral, obsessive and hysterical personality, self-actualization and death anxiety. The results indicated that none of the personality variables significantly related to death anxiety. The personality variables tended to relate negatively to self-actualization. Death anxiety was not related to self-actualization.

49. Vargo, M. E. & Batsel Jr., W. M. (1981). Relationship between death anxiety and components of the self-actualization process. Psychological Reports, 48(1), 89-90.

Reports an inverse relationship in a study of nursing students between fear of death and self-actualization.

50. Wood, K. & Robinson, P. J. (1982). Actualization and the fear of death: Retesting an existential hypotheses. Essence: Issues in the Study of ageing, Dying, and Death, 5(3), 235-243.

Demonstrates "that within a group of highly actualized individuals, the degree to which "own death" is integrated into constructs of self is a far more powerful predictor of fear of death than actualization."

Dissertations and Theses

51. Gamble, J. W. (1974). The relationship of self-actualization and authenticity to the experience of mortality. DAI, 35(7), 3578B.

52. Garrison, P. H. M. (1984) A comparison of registered nurses who work with terminally ill patients in a hospice and those who do not work on death anxiety, self-actualization, and selected personal, social, and professional variables. DAI, 46(5), 1511B.

53. Katz, S. I. (1978). The relationship of the mid-life transition to death anxiety and self-actualization. DAI. 39(8), 4035B.

54. Klug, L. F. (1976). <u>An empirical investigation of the relationship between self-actualization and reconciliation with death.</u> Unpublished doctoral dissertation, University of Ottawa, Canada.

55. Pollak, J. M. (1977). Relationships between obsessive personality, death anxiety, and self-actualization. <u>DAI</u>, <u>38</u>(2), 637A.

56. Steele, R. S. (1979). Self actualization and death confrontation. <u>DAI</u>,<u>40</u>(3), 1387B.

57. Stevens, M. A. (1982). The effects of a death awareness workshop on self-actualization and death anxiety. <u>DAI</u>, <u>43</u>(5), 1600D.

58. Strauss, W. C. (1977). <u>Widowhood: Self-actualization, death anxiety, and integration of life and death concepts.</u> Unpublished doctoral dissertation, California School of Professional Psychology, Fresno, California.

59. Wesch, J. E. (1971) Self-actualization and fear of death. <u>DAI</u>, <u>31</u>(10), 6270-6271B.

60. Wexler, J. R. (1978). Death threat, self-actualization and future-time orientation. <u>DAI</u>, <u>39</u>(3), 1507B.

The field of education has been one of the most impacted by theories, writing and research concerning self-actualization. Research and writing on self-actualization in education is wide-ranging concerning itself with the goals of education, the curriculum, the psychological health of teachers and students and even the materials produced. The studies of the educational process include the investigation of such daily interactions as contact between teachers and students, residence hall living and concerns with discipline. The writings on self-actualization stand in stark contrast to the writings of behaviorism, religious fundamentalism and back-to-basics. The writings reveal that there is more speculation than fact and the educational institution can still profit from well-considered, well-conducted educational experiments using self-actualization theory as a basis.

61. Beach, F. H. (1975, Summer). The myth of self-actualization for the gifted. North Carolina Association for the Gifted and Talented Quarterly, 1(3), 35-38.

Argues that the gifted child has a need for self-actualization in direct proportion to cognitive abilities. The article makes a plea for increasing the emphasis placed on meeting the affective needs of the gifted and talented.

62. Beittel, K. R. (1979, November). The teaching of art in relation to body-mind integration and self-actualization in art. Art Education, 32(7), 18-20.

Describes a point of view in the teaching of art which employs Eastern concepts in which it is suggested that when "we truly teach art, we are mediating body-mind integration and self-

actualization in and through art." The author
summarizes the three points of the article as:
"(1) wholistic participation of the body-mind
is both precursor and outcome of growth and
self-actualization; (2) growth and self-
actualization are organic processes requiring
a special kind of language for both their
nurturance and for understanding them; and (3)
this language, in its very infancy, is a
dialectical, metaphorical one which I have
termed the language of practice."

63. Bledsoe Jr., G. M. (1975, September). Self-
actualization: The purpose of education.
NASSP Bulletin, 59(392), 88-93.

Suggests that many school problems would
disappear if the goal of school were self-
actualization. The author says that an
individually developed curriculum for each
student which emphasized respect, excellence,
receptivity, efficiency in learning, critical
thinking, accurate observation and creativity
would promote the maximum growth of students,
lead to self-actualization and prevent
discipline problems in schools.

64. Borowy, T. D. & McGuire, J. M. (1983, June).
Experiential versus didactic teaching: Changes
in self-actualization. Journal of Humanistic
Education and Development, 21(4), 146-152.

Reports research investigating differences in
outcome between direct teaching and direct
experiences in promoting self-actualization.
This study investigated the personal benefits
of experience rather than academic outcomes.
In general, experiential outcomes were
superior to direct teaching.

65. Cangemi, J. P. (1984, Winter). The real
purpose of higher education: Developing self-
actualizing personalities. Education, 105(2),
151-154.

Studied the responses of students, professors
and administrators regarding how they
perceived self-actualization as the major

purpose of higher education. The results were that all groups were in general agreement that the overall purpose of higher education was to help all associated with it move toward self-actualization.

66. Cangemi, J. P. (1975, April-May). Self-actualizing behavior: A goal for student personnel services. College Student Journal, 9(2), 141-143.

Recommends that a purpose of student personnel services be the development of self-actualization in college students. While the author does not suggest that full self-actualization could occur in the college experience, he does suggest that "developing the process of moving toward the direction of self-actualization is an objective that can be obtained during the collegiate experience."

67. Cares, R. C. & Blackburn, R. T. (1978, October). Faculty self-actualization: Factors affecting career success. Research in Higher Education, 9(2), 123-136.

Investigated factors affecting higher education faculty growth, development and satisfaction. Generally, the results indicate that perceived control of the environment and ability to be involved in decision-making increased feelings of satisfaction. The authors suggest that these factors lie within the ability of administrators to change and recommend that attention be paid to these factors as well as other goals in faculty develop programs.

68. Coble, C. R. (1973). Self-actualization and the effective biology teacher. American Biology Teacher, 35, 479-481.

Sought to determine if positive changes in critical thinking in biology students could be related to higher self-actualization in their teachers. Teachers of students with increased critical thinking abilities were significantly higher on several aspects of self-actualization than teachers of students with negative or no change in critical thinking ability.

69. Coble, C. R. & Hounshell, P. B. (1972, July-September). Teacher self-actualization and student progress. Science Education, 56(3), 311-316.

"Utilizing analysis of covariance, no significant differences could be found between mean gains in critical thinking and biology achievement for student of SA(self-actualizing), N(normal), NSA(not self-actualizing) biology teachers." (parenthesis ours). "Biology teachers re-grouped on the basis of significant gains (Group I) versus nonsignificant gains (Group II) in the critical thinking abilities of their students, revealed significant differences in the self-actualizing characteristics of the effective and ineffective teachers." (parenthesis theirs).

70. Combs, A. W. (1972, Fall). Administration and the adequate personality. Colorado Journal of Educational Research, 12(1), 24-27.

Presents a theoretical case that the tensions and stresses of administration lie not in the job itself but in the administrator. The article reviews research and principles which point to three major areas: (1) the administrator; (2) the administrator's view of other people; and (3) the relationship between the two. Finally, the author argues that the adequate personality overcomes the stresses and tensions of the job through attitudes described in the article.

71. Dandes, H. M. (1966, Fall). Psychological health and teaching effectiveness. Journal of Teacher Education, 17(3), 301-306.

Presents a study comparing self-actualization of teachers to values related to effective teaching. The results show a significant relationship between measured self-actualization and the selected attitudes and values of effective teaching. Makes a case that "those who are concerned with increasing the effectiveness of teachers must consider modifying the college curriculum to include experiences which will aid the potential teacher to grow and develop psychologically, {and} to actualize..."

72. Darou, W. G. (1982, September). Reaction to "increase in assertiveness and actualization as a function of didactic training." Journal of Counseling Psychology, 29(5), 542.

Refers to article by Goddard (82) in which the author challenges the conclusion of that article that self-actualization is increased by didactic training by arguing that didactic training changes knowledge about self-actualization not self-actualization itself. See also (81).

73. Deibert, J. P. & Hoy, W. K. (1977, Summer). "Custodial" high school and self-actualization of students. Educational Research Quarterly, 2(2), 24-31.

Studied the relationship between pupil control strategy of the high school and student self-actualization. "As hypothesized, the results indicated that the more custodial the pupil control orientation of the school, the less inner directed, time competent, and self-actualized the student body."

74. Deming, A. L. (1980, March). Self-actualization level as predictor of practicum supervision effectiveness. Journal of Counseling Psychology, 27(2), 213-216.

Researched the relationship between growth in self-actualization in counseling practicum students and level of self-actualization of the supervisor. The hypothesis that high self-actualizing supervisors would promote greater growth in practicum students was not supported. All students gained in self-actualization in the practicum.

Self-Actualization

75. Doggett, M. (1974, May). A self-actualization process of teachers. ERIC Document, ED 100 823.

Object was to develop and evaluate a process of self-actualization for teachers. The author reports that gains were made by all teachers in the directions of self-actualization and that the 8 step process seems applicable for all levels of teaching. The Manual includes descriptions of the 8 steps and an appendix with "teacher evaluation forms, ratings of the teacher from the perspective of the teacher and the principal, a growth chart, and a survey of self-actualization."

76. Doyle, J. A. (1976, June). Congruent self-concepts and psychological health of college students. Psychological Reports, 38(3, Pt 2), 1257-1258.

Investigated the relationship between ideal self-image and self-actualization. The results indicate "evidence of a small to moderate positive relationship between measures of self-ideal congruity and psychological health qua self-actualization."

77. Drews, E. M. (1966). Self-actualization: A new focus for education. In W. Waetjen (Ed.) Learning and mental health in the school. Washington, D.C.:Association for Supervision and Curriculum Development.

Promotes self-actualization as a focus for education and provides the reader with criticisms of current educational practices as well as a design for an experimental program based on self-actualization with assumptions, content, materials and ideas about children to provide an underpinning for humanistic education.

78. Eisner, V. (1972, Spring). A self-realization workshop for upward bound students. People Watching, 1(1) 23-27.

Provides an account of a "beginning

21

Psychology" class for upward bound students aimed at "self-realization" and reports in detail a unit on creativity. The author provides evaluations of the class by the students, references for the creativity unit and a model for developing other units.

79. Farmer, R. (1984, Winter). Humanistic education and self-actualization theory. Education, 105(2), 162-172.

Argues that Maslow's theory can provide the basis for humanistic education.

80. Farmer, R. B. (1980, September-October). Self-actualization and the effective social studies teacher. Social Studies, 71(5), 231-236.

Purpose of the study was to investigate the relationship between teachers of social studies self-actualization and effectiveness. The results for groups indicate that "(1) degree of teacher self-actualization is positively and significantly related to effective teacher cognitive behavior of the secondary social studies teachers. (2) degree of self-actualization in combination with increasing teacher age and increasing teacher religious nonfundamentalism are significantly and positively related to effective teacher cognitive behavior."

81. Fox, J. V. D. (1965). The self-actualizing teacher. Improving College and University Teaching, 13, 147-148.

Promotes the idea that greatness in teaching does not lie in the methods used by teachers but in their capacity for self-examination, growth and self-actualization. The author argues that the purpose of education is the self-actualization of students and that teachers should personify the concept.

82. Glatthorn, A. A. (1969, March). Individual self-fulfillment in the large high school. NASSP Bulletin, 53(335), 47-56.

Develops the theme that "each learner is unique; that each youngster has some undeveloped potential, some special self which only [that youngster] can become; and that the job of the school is to deploy all its resources - curriculum, staff, materials, schedules - to facilitate this self-fulfillment.

83. Goddard, R. C. (1982, September). Comment on "reaction to 'increase in assertiveness and actualization as a function of didactic training'." Journal of Counseling Psychology, 29(5), 543-544.

Refers to article (70) in which it is suggested that effects of previous research (82) were due to an increase in knowledge about self-actualization rather than self-actualization alone is not supported by other research.

84. Goddard, R. C. (1981, July). Increase in assertiveness and actualization as a function of didactic training. Journal of Counseling Psychology, 28(4), 279-287.

Study attempted to determine whether didactic training could increase assertiveness and self-actualization. The researchers divided non-assertive undergraduates into groups which received video tapes presenting didactic principles of Rogerian therapy and assertiveness. The results indicate that there was a positive significant change for groups in self-actualization for both didactic training in Rogerian therapy and assertiveness. However, no change was observed in assertiveness as a result of didactic training.

85. Goldman, J. A. (1978, March-April). Effect of a faculty development workshop upon self-actualization. Education, 98(3), 254-258.

Studied the effect of a staff development workshop on self-actualization. In general, the results were that faculty who attended the workshop increased their scores on a measure of self-actualization. The workshop encompassed personal, instructional and organizational components.

86. Goldman, J. A. & Olczak, P. V. (1980). Effect of an innovative educational program upon self-actualization and psychosocial maturity: A replication and follow up. Social Behavior and Personality, 8(1), 41-47.

Replicated (87) to determine if the unexpected results would be maintained and to follow up the previous group. The previous results were repeated and there were no significant differences in the follow up.

87. Goldman, J. A. & Olczak, P. V. (1976, May). Effect of an innovative academic program upon self-actualization and psychosocial maturity. Journal of Educational Research, 69(9), 333-337.

Compared students in an innovative academic program with students not enrolled in the program. The results were unexpected in that the participants in the program went down in self-actualization scores while the non-participants went up. See (86).

88. Graff, R. W. & Bradshaw, H. E. (1970). Relationship of a measure of self-actualization to dormitory assistant effectiveness. Journal of Counseling Psychology, 17(6), 502-505.

Investigated the relationship of a self-actualization measure to rating of dormitory assistants by students and personnel deans. The results showed that the Personality Orientation Inventory (POI) may have some usefulness as a selection tool for dormitory assistants.

89. Griggs, M. B. (1972, March-April). Self-actualization through vocational education. Illinois Teacher for Contemporary Roles, 15(4), 151-154.

Advocates vocational education, as opposed to vocational training, as a way to help students attain the knowledge they need to make sound career decisions and as one other path to self-actualization.

90. Hampton, J. D. & Kerasotes, D. L. (1979, Winter). Faculty level of self-actualization in relation to student rating of instructors. Educational and Psychological Measurement, 39(4), 971-975.

Attempted to explain why students rated instructors differently using a university approved instructor rating form and a measure of self-actualization. The results indicated only one positive significant correlation. The time competence scale on the self-actualization measure and positive student ratings. It was suggested that organized instructional patterns might account for this correlation.

91. Henjum, A. (1983, Fall). Let's select "self-actualizing" teachers. Education, 104(1), 51-55.

Makes a plea for identifying and employing teachers who are self-actualizing and employing them in the schools as a way of improving education. The author supports this desire by indicating that both students and supervising teachers gave the highest rating to student teachers who were self-actualizing.

92. Huntsman, K. H. (1982, April). Improvisational dramatic activities: Key to self-actualization. Children's Theatre Review, 31(2), 3-9.

Investigated whether improvisational drama experience had an effect on the self-confidence, self-worth, spontaneity, ability to relate to others and, in a word, self-actualization of students enrolled in the class. Overall, the results suggested tendencies in the direction of improvement for all categories.

93. Husa, H. E. (1978, June). Self-actualization in an education psychology course for college freshman honors students. Psychological Reports, 42(3, Pt 2), 1333-1334.

Reports a study in which self-awareness and exploratory exercises were used in an undergraduate honors educational psychology class to promote self-actualization. A post-test revealed that the scores of students in the class were comparable to self-actualized norms.

94. Ivie, S. D. (1982, September-October). Self-actualization: Its use and misuse in teacher education. Journal of Teacher Education, 33(5), 24-27.

Argues that self-actualization has no practical use for teacher education even though it may be an interesting theory in psychology.

95. Johnson, N., Russo, C., & Bundrick, C. M. (1982, September). Rational behavioral training and changes in self-actualization. Journal of Specialists in Group Work, 7(3), 187-193.

Measured the effect of a rational behavioral training group on the self-actualization of the participants. The results of the study indicated significant positive changes toward self-actualization after the training.

96. Jury, L. E., Willower, D. J. & DeLacy, W. J. (1975, December). Teacher self-actualization and pupil control ideology. Alberta Journal of Educational Research, 21(4), 295-301.

Predicted that teacher level of self-actualization would be directly related to a humanistic orientation toward pupil control ideology. This was supported and it was further observed that level of self-actualization was not significantly different for sex, grade level taught or experience. See also Noll, Willower and Barnette (112).

97. Kramer, M., McDonnel, C., & Reed, J. L. (1972, March-April). Self-actualization and role adaption of baccalaureate degree nurses. Nursing Research, 21(3), 111-123

    Studied self-actualization and role adaptation among a sample of baccalaureate degree nurses. Nurses who are successful seem to be on the road to self-actualization and also have a high loyalty to the bureaucratic work system. However, nurses who seem to have trouble are nurses who are not moving toward self-actualization and still hold high work values.

98. Lambert, M. J., Segger, J. F., Stanley, J. S.,Spencer, B., and Nelson, D. (1978). Reported self-concept and self-actualizing value changes as a function of academic classes with wilderness experience. Perceptual and Motor Skills, 46(3), 1035-1040.

    Studied changes in self-concept and self-actualization resulting from a wilderness experience. The study compared two types of wilderness experiences to a lecture class. The results indicated changes in self-concept from the wilderness experience but no change in self-actualization. The lecture class produced no changes in either measure.

99. Leib, J. W. & Snyder, W. U. (1968). Achievement and positive mental health. Journal of Counseling Psychology, 15, 388-389.

    Studied the relationship between a measure of self-actualization and achievement. The results failed to show any relationship between self-actualization and achievement. See also (100) and (101).

100. Leib, J. W. & Snyder, W. U. (1967). Effects of group discussions on underachievement and self-actualization. Journal of Counseling Psychology, 14(3), 282-285.

    Investigated the effect of a discussion group versus a lecture group on grade point average and self-actualization. The results showed

27

significant increases in self-actualization scores and grade point average for underachieving students for both the discussion group and the lecture group. The authors suggest that the special attention given in both groups accounts for improvements. See also (99) and (101).

101. LeMay, M. L. (1969, November). Self-actualization and college achievement at three ability levels. Journal of Counseling Psychology, 16(6), 582-583.

Attempted to clarify early studies by Leib and Snyder (99 & 100) in which somewhat different results occurred. This study resulted in some support of the Leib and Snyder study (99) and revealed intellectual ability may act as a moderator variable in the relationship between self-actualization and achievement.

102. LeMay, M. L. & Damm, V. J. (1968, Summer). The personal orientation inventory as a measure of the self-actualization of underachievers. Measurement and Evaluation in Guidance, 1(2), 110-114.

Investigated the value orientation of college freshmen underachievers who volunteered for academic and personal counseling. It was proposed that underachievement would be significantly and negatively related to self-actualization. "The data show that the Personal Orientation Inventory (POI) did successfully differentiate the academically successful subjects ... from the underachievers. However, the small sample of the study prevent more than a general statement regarding the usefulness of this instrument for use in identifying underachievers."

103. Malanowski, J. R. & Wood, P. H. (1984, May). Burnout and self-actualization in public school teachers. Journal of Psychology, 117(1), 23-26.

Studied burnout and self-actualization among public school teachers. The results were that the sub-scales of the burnout inventory ranged from a negative correlation to a very low positive correlation. Thus, it was concluded that higher self-actualizing teachers tended to resist burnout better than teachers who scored low on a measure of self-actualization.

104. Maslow, A. H. (1968, Fall). Some educational implications of the humanistic psychologies. Harvard Educational Review, 38(4), 685-696.

Presents, in more detail than in any other of his articles, Maslow's views on education and explores the role of peak experiences and, in general, the place of self-actualization in the schools.

105. McAlindon, H. R. (1981, October). Education for self-actualization. Training and Development Journal, 35(10), 85-91.

Presents an argument for changes in the schools based on 7 propositions which the author believes will have to change to guide the schools in the future. These "educational shifts" are: teach self-esteem and self-respect, integrate the art "making a living" and the art "living a meaningful life," from "what to think" to "how to think," "self-directed learning," emphasize quality and excellence in the curriculum, from studying "what was said" to "what can be," and self-actualization.

106. McClain, E. W. & Andrews, H. B. (1972, November). Self-actualization among extremely superior students. Journal of College Student Personnel, 13(6), 505-510.

Attempted to make a broad assessment of the self-actualization of college seniors already identified as extremely superior in terms of their academic achievements. The study revealed different patterns of self-actualization mostly revolving around academic pursuits for superior students who were lacking in fulfilling interpersonal relationships.

107. Morris, G. B. (1979, February). Teacher's attitudes in relation to rational-emotive and self-actualization theories. Psychological Reports, 44(1), 229-230.

Investigated teacher trainees' teaching attitudes, rational beliefs and self-actualization. The results indicate that " college students with positive attitudes towards teaching were considered to be present-oriented, inner-directed, and spontaneous. They possessed self-actualization values, had positive feelings toward self and others, and showed rational thinking."

108. Mullins, R. F. & Perkins, E. M. (1973, January). Increased self-actualization as a result of an intensive one semester academic program. Journal of Educational Research, 66(5), 210-214.

Investigated the effects of an innovative biology program which stressed applications of biology to social problems. The results indicated that students gained overall on a measure of self-actualization especially in the areas of inner directedness and acceptance of aggression in themselves.

109. Murray, E. (1972, Fall). Students' perceptions of self-actualizing and non-self-actualizing teachers. Journal of Teacher Education, 23(3), 383-387.

Studied two samples of teachers, one high and one low in self-actualization, to determine if students viewed self-actualizing teachers differently than non-self-actualizing teachers. The results showed clear differences between the groups with the self-actualizing teachers being viewed more positively.

Self-Actualization

110. Newell, G. E. (1977, November). The emerging self: A curriculum of self-actualization. English Journal, 66(8), 32-34.

Presents a curriculum that is student-centered, question-centered and language centered based on personal experience as a 9th grade English teacher of non-college bound students. The author attempts to build a curriculum that addresses here-and-now concerns of students aimed at self-actualization.

111. Noad, R. (1979, February). Maslow's need hierarchy related to educational attitudes and self-concepts of elementary student teachers. Educational Review, 31(1), 51-57.

Investigated relationships among Maslow's need hierarchy, educational attitudes and self-concepts of elementary student teachers. The results indicate that self-concept and attitude toward teaching were related to motivation. The author states that "educational attitudes and self-concept, operating jointly, significantly contributed to the variance in Maslow's needs hierarchy scales of basic, safety and self-actualization needs."

112. Noll, R. L., Willower, D. J. & Barnette, J. J. (1977, March). Teacher self-actualization and pupil control ideology-behavior consistency. Alberta Journal of Educational Research, 23(1), 65-70.

Builds upon previous study of Jury, Willower and DeLacy (96) which reported teacher humanism directly related to pupil control ideology. This study investigated the "hypothesis that teacher level of self-actualization would predict the consistency between teacher pupil control ideology and behavior." The hypothesis was supported. However, there was a reported difference between teacher ideology and behavior.

113. Nolte, A. (1976, May-June). The relevance of Abraham Maslow's work to health education. Health Education, 7(3), 25-27.

Informs the reader of the background and some of the publications of Abraham Maslow as they contribute to health education. The article outlines how Maslow's work contributes a philosophical perspective to health education. Additionally, the author identifies how Maslow's work can contribute to professional preparation concerns as well as curricular decisions.

114. Omizo, M. M. (1981, March). A study of self-actualization and facilitative communication. Humanist Educator, 19(3), 116-125.

"Study was conducted to determine (a) the relationship between self-actualization measures and ability in facilitative communication of trainees from counseling, social work, and psychology graduate program and (b) if differences exist among the three groups of mental health trainees relative to self-actualization and ability in facilitative communication measures." The results indicate that persons with higher self-actualization scores also tended to have better facilitative communication skills.

115. Ost, D. H. (1973, October-December). The nature of science, self-actualization, and science teacher education. Science Education, 57(4), 521-524.

Argues for an approach to science education and science teaching that emphasize choice, freedom and humanism. The author believes that problems in science education have come from the neglect of the human qualities and treating science as a group of different disciplines.. The article advocates the importance of choice, self-evaluation and a synthetic approach to science teacher as important in leading to self-actualization.

Self-Actualization

116. Porter, C. M. (1979, March). Self-actualization, liberalism, and humanistic education. Humanist Educator, 17(3), 111-118.

Studied the relationship between self-actualization and liberal-conservative values. The author concludes from the study that the contention that in order to promote self-actualization in others one must be self-actualizing is false. Further, the connection between liberal values and self-actualization was not supported in this study.

117. Proefriedt, W. (1983, Winter). Self-fulfillment and educational reform. Teachers College Record, 85(2), 205-224.

Attacks a number of educational reform documents as being based on "cold war" ideologies simply presenting their recommendations in metaphors of military and industrial language and as well as criticizing the tendency to advocate "standards" and "excellence" "within a context of fear at the loss of American military and educational preeminence" without any "critical reflection on the larger purposes of our schools and society."

118. Richards, F. (1972, Fall). Counselor training: Educating for the beautiful and noble person. Colorado Journal of Educational Research, 12(1), 11-16.

Advocates a process of education for counselors that would be "a model of the counselor or helper as one becoming fully human, fully growing and fully functioning in every aspect of ... life."

119. Sands, B. L. (1971, February). Relationship between family life teachers' self-actualization and self-perception of competency. Journal of Home Economics, 63(2), 113-115.

Studied teachers self-perception of competency and relationship to self-actualization. An unpredicted outcome was some evidence that age is not related to self-actualization. The results of the study show some relationship between teachers' personal and professional competences.

120. Sandven, J. (1976). Self-realization at school: An explorative study about causes of lack of self-realization. Scandinavian Journal of Educational Research, 20(2), 85-102.

Investigates the obvious discrepancy between students potential and progress at school. The author reports on research material on approximately 3500 students that was analyzed for lack of achievement and its possible causes. While no single cause was identified, the author characterizes the lack of self-realization as due to teachers' judging future possibilities by achievement rather than by potential and students doing exactly the same. Thus, the author says self-image is may be the most basic factor in lack of self-realization.

121. Schroeder, C. C. & LeMay, M. L. (1973). The impact of coed residence halls on self-actualization. Journal of College Student Personnel, 14(2), 105-110.

Calls for more research on the topic of coed residence halls while in general supporting the hypothesis that such living arrangement promote better male-female relationships and movement toward self-actualization.

122. Sluyter, G. V. & Cleland, C. C. (1972, August). Self-actualization among institutional personnel. Training School Bulletin, 69(2), 83-91.

Researched the level of self-actualization of employees of two large residential treatment facilities at different hierarchical job levels. The results indicate that overall job satisfaction is similar for all levels of the hierarchy. However, it was noted that different needs were apparent for persons at different levels of the job hierarchy.

123. Stern, G. G. (1971, November). Self-actualizing environments for students. School Review, 80(1), 1-25.

Presents an argument that colleges tend to divided themselves into two types. "One involves processes associated with participants' self-actualization; the other, various controls for maintaining group structure." The author suggest that students often self-select themselves into one or the other. The author concludes that "people do appear to exercise a preference for being treated as subject or as object...but there is no reason to believe that the experience of learning to be themselves should be denied to anyone..." The author argues that there can be no "defense for learning environments that are coercive or demeaning."

124. Thiebe, E. H. (1972, November). Technology serves self-realization. Music Educators Journal, 59(3), 34-35.

Advocates and presents and example of how technology can serve to meet the individual needs of children in music and help promote self-realization.

125. Turrall, G. (1971, June). Total development of the individual through continuing education. Canadian Counsellor, 5(3), 195-196.

Advocates, for certain types of students, who are involved in degree programs, a system in which credit is awarded for experience directly related to specific course requirements.

126. Van Gorder, E. & Kemerer, F. R. (1972, October). Values and decision making: Helping students achieve self-actualization. Independent School Bulletin, 31(1), 26-31.

Reprint of (127) below.

127. Van Gorder, E. & Kemerer, F. R. (1971, July). Helping students achieve self-actualization: A case study of non-directed college counseling. National ACAC Journal, 16(2), 11-15.

Argues that whether to attend college and then which college to attend is a matter for the student and the student alone to decide. The article then presents a case study of how this process might take place.

128. Welch, I. D. & Rodwick, R. (1972, Fall). Communicating the sciences: The scientist as a healthy personality. Colorado Journal of Education Research, 12(1), 6-10.

Describes characteristics of the healthy personality from several different theories. The authors present an argument that the characteristics of healthy personality are just the characteristics needed for effective and productive scientists.

129. Wexler, D. A. (1974, February). Self-actualization and cognitive processes. Journal of Consulting and Clinical Psychology, 42(1), 47-53.

"Investigated the hypotheses that (a) the creation of new experience in cognitive functioning involves increased differentiation and integration of meaning and (b) self-actualization involves the tendency to engage in a mode of cognitive processing that creates new experience." The results indicate that a high level of cognitive complexity is an aspect of high level psychological well-being.

130. Young, R. A. & Crandall, R. (1984).
Wilderness use and self-actualization.
Journal of Leisure Research, 16(2), 149-160.

     Sought to establish a relationship between
     self-actualization and wilderness use. Self-
     actualization was found to be related to
     wilderness attitudes. Self-actualization was
     more highly related to wilderness users than
     non-users. However, the authors conclude
     that the relationship between self-
     actualization and wilderness use was weak.

131. Zimmerman, K. W. & Scruggs, M. M. (1979,
March). Classroom verbal interaction and
self-actualization of home economics
teachers. Home Economics Research Journal,
7(4), 219-225.

     Purpose of the study was to analyze verbal
     interaction in classroom discussions with
     measured self-actualization. Self-
     actualizing teachers tended to vary more in
     verbal patterns than non-self-actualizing
     teachers.

132. Zimmerman, K. W. & Scruggs, M. M. (1978,
November). Self-actualization of teachers
and teacher-student rapport. Home Economics
Research Journal, 7(2), 128-134.

     Multi-purposed study aimed at the
     relationship between background
     characteristics and self-actualization, to
     develop a teacher-student rapport instrument
     and to investigate differences in teacher-
     student rapport between teachers with
     differing levels of self-actualization. The
     background characteristics were not related
     to degree of self-actualization. No
     significant differences were identified
     between the two groups of teachers.

Dissertations and Theses

133. Allen, B. E. (1972). Relationships between academic achievement, social intelligence, self-actualization and teaching methods. Unpublished doctoral dissertation, University of Southern California, Los Angeles.

134. Armstrong, G. (1982). The effects of a structured and unstructured group approach on the perceptual accuracy, empathy, and self-actualization of first year human services students. DAI, 43(3), 640A.

135. Arulefela, O. A. (1984). A study of the relationship of self-actualization and job satisfaction of certain categories of secondary school teachers in the Nigerian states of Ondo, Oyo and Ogun. DAI, 45(5), 1248A.

136. Ayers Jr., L. W. (1975). The effects of a summer instituted for cultural awareness on the measured level of self-actualization of experienced teachers. DAI, 36(5), 2747A.

137. Bagott, N. A. (1968). Student-teacher's decisions in interactive situations related to degree of self-actualization. DAI, 30(3), 1038A.

138. Baillie, W. R. (1980). The effects of an experiential undergraduate teacher education program on the development of self actualization. DAI, 41(7), 2906A.

139. Balog, T. G. (1984). The relationship of measures of self-actualization to nursing competency of students completing an associate degree career mobility nursing program. DAI, 45(5), 1428B.

140. Barrar, A. K. (1982). A correlation study between self-actualization of teachers and students' evaluations of their teaching effectiveness. DAI, 44(2), 367A.

Self-Actualization

141. Baum, R. (1975). Teacher self-actualization and dogmatism as related to students' perceptions of teaching behaviors. DAI, 36(9), 6006A.

142. Bell, P. A. (1977). Motivation to attend college related to level of self-actualization and scholastic aptitude scores of entering college students. DAI, 38(5), 2612A.

143. Biondolillo, A. C. (1973). A study of the differences in self-actualization and job satisfaction between individually prescribed instruction teachers and traditional teachers. DAI, 34(10), 6285A.

144. Bird, S. W. (1979). The relationships among perceptual characteristics, self-actualization, and teaching effectiveness in developmental studies instructors and non-developmental studies instructors in selected community colleges. DAI, 41(1), 77A.

145. Bishop, J. E. (1983). Effects of "ounce" classroom management training on the self-esteem, self-actualization and burnout of elementary school teachers. DAI, 44(7), 2088A.

146. Bjorkqvist, B. O. J. (1981). The effect of methods courses emphasizing self-actualization and basic competencies on anxiety specific to the teaching of physical science at the elementary level. DAI, 42(11). 4795A.

147. Borchard, D. C. (1976). Self-actualization in Vietnam veteran and non-veteran male college students. DAI, 37(8), 4975A.

148. Boston, B. D. (1975). Self-actualization as a predictor of teaching success in individually guided education. DAI, 35(4), 2093A.

149. Bouverat, R. A. (1970). A study of self-actualization and perceptions of teaching roles of prospective teachers of young children. DAI, 32(1), 85A.

150. Bowman, B. C. (1974). Predictors of measured self-actualization among university professors. DAI, 35(7), 3548B.

151. Bowlan, B. N. (1972). Relationship between self-actualization and perceived effectiveness among principals and teachers. DAI, 33(8), 4235A.

152. Boyd, G. S. (1972). The relationship of a summer collegiate experience by high school students in certain louisiana colleges and university to the development of self-actualization as measured by the Personal Orientation Inventory. DAI, 33(7), 3367A.

153. Brunner, J. C. (1971). Organizational variables and teacher self-actualization in public and private schools. DAI, 32(10), 5488A.

154. Burdg, M. L. (1970). Relationship of student attrition rates and self-actualization of community college teachers. DAI, 31(5), 2169.

155. Cangemi, J. P. (1974). Perceptions of students, faculty and administrators regarding self-actualization as the purpose of higher education. DAI, 35(9), 5844A.

156. Cares, R. C. (1975). Self-actualization attitudes of faculty and their perceptions of their career success. DAI, 36(10), 6543A.

157. Chase, L. G. (1978). The development of a training program to facilitate the self-actualization of teachers. DAI, 39(12), 7234A.

158. Chedekel, D. S. (1971). The levels of anxiety and self-actualization in dropout-prone ninth grade boys. DAI, 32(4), 1847A.

Self-Actualization

159. Coble, C. R. (1971). An analysis of the relationship between the biology teacher's level of self-actualization and student progress. DAI, 32(5), 2503A.

160. Collins, R. N. (1971). A study of the relationship between health knowledge, self-actualization and classroom verbal behavior of secondary school health student-teachers. Unpublished doctoral dissertation, University of Oregon, Eugene, Oregon.

161. Curley, M. M. (1982). Job satisfaction and self-actualization characteristics of curriculum developers. DAI, 43(6), 1812A.

162. Curtis, S. A. The effects of personal development education on growth toward self-actualization: An empirical analysis. DAI, 40(10), 5331A.

163. Danyluk, J. J. (1981). Interrelationship between secondary school principals' level of self-actualization leadership attitude, and teacher perception of principal leadership behavior. Unpublished doctoral dissertation, University of Alberta, Canada.

164. Deibert, J. P. (1977). Pupil control ideology of teachers and student self-actualization in the public schools. DAI, 38(7), 3829A.

165. DiSciullo, M. A. (1981). Factors influencing chronic absenteeism in two Suffolk County schools in New York State. DAI, 41(12), 5049A.

166. Doyle, E. J. (1969). The relationship between college teacher effectiveness and inferred characteristics of the adequate personality. DAI, 30(10), 4774B.

167. Durka, D. W. (1973). Self-actualization and internal control in nursing students. DAI, 35(1), 254A.

168. Durschmidt, B. J. H. (1977). Self-actualization and the human potential group process in a community college. DAI, 38(7), 3953A.

169. Edwards, V. B. (1983). Relationship between self-actualization and teaching effectiveness in selected groups of community college instructors. DAI, 44(12), 3584A.

170. Eiden, J. A. (1973). The relationship between self-actualization and selected learning experiences of elementary education majors enrolled in the University of North Dakota's Center for Teaching and Learning. DAI, 34(8), 4954A.

171. Fales, A. W. (1975). Self-actualization motivation and continuing professional education in a sample of engineers. DAI, 36(12), 7805A.

172. Farmer, R. B. (1978). The relationship between social studies teacher self-actualization and teacher effectiveness. DAI, 39(10), 5900A.

173. Feichtner, S. H. (1972). Design of a student-teaching experience based on a theory of self-actualization. DAI, 34(1), 208A.

174. Fellenz, R. A. (1972). An approach to the evaluation of self-actualization occurring in selected adult education participants. DAI, 33(1), 135A.

175. Finn, M. (1979). The effects of systematic human relations training on self-actualization and clinical effectiveness of undergraduate students in communication disorders. DAI, 40(9), 4240B.

176. Finney, B. J. (1980). Self-actualization and need for autonomy of adult and traditional-age students at Kansas State university. DAI, 41(5), 1894A.

Self-Actualization

177. Ford, S. S. (1978). The relationship of self-actualization to measures of academic success. DAI, 39(11), 6500A.

178. Frederick, A. H. (1974). Self-actualization and personality type: A comparative study of doctoral majors in educational administration and the helping relations. DAI, 35(11), 7055A.

179. Gibb, L. L. (1966). A study of differences in sex, home background, educational background, work experience, extra-curricular participation, and self-actualization attainment in college juniors. DAI, 27(8), 2358A.

180. Goins, P. N. (1977). A study of self-actualization and education in registered nurses. DAI, 38(11), 5279B.

181. Graham, J. D. (1980). The effect of counseling with the career decision kit on the self-actualization of college students who seek career counseling. DAI, 41(6), 2449A.

182. Green, E. J. (1967). The relationship of self-actualization to achievement in nursing. DAI, 28(6), 2092A.

183. Greer, J. F. (1974). The effects of two teaching styles and internal-external control on self-actualization and language achievement in gifted adolescents. DAI, 35(7), 4147A.

184. Grossman, B. B. (1976). Relationship of task-orientation and self-actualization to role perception and commitment to teaching in preservice teachers. DAI, 37(4), 2122A.

185. Hartleib, C. J. (1978). The impact of an interpersonal coping skills program on the personal competencies and self-actualization levels of social service students. DAI, 40(2), 753A.

Self-Actualization

186. Hartsell, J. E. (1975). The effects of competition in learning in public schools on the self-actualization process. DAI, 36(9), 5861A.

187. Hawkins, H. H. (1979). The development and evaluation of a mental health course and its relationship to changes in self-concept, autonomy, and self-actualization. DAI, 40(11), 5739A.

188. Heggoy, S. J. (1985). Motivation and the learning disabled college student: A qualitative study. DAI, 46(7), 1901A.

189. Heintschel, R. M. (1978). An analysis of the relationship between science teacher self-actualization and science student attitude and achievement. DAI, 39(6), 3501A.

190. Henderson, D. B. (1976). Identification and analysis of the relationship between self-actualization and leadership style in selected graduate students in educational administration. DAI, 37(8), 4894A.

191. Hines, C. C. W. (1978). The relationship of the actualizing process and the human potential seminar to the self-concept and self-actualization of community college students. DAI, 39(5), 2755A.

192. Hogan, W. J. (1980). An investigation of the relationship between self-actualization, self-perception, and student evaluated teacher performance of university faculty. DAI, 41(9), 3806A.

193. Holt, D. D. (1972). An analysis of the relationship between student teachers' self-actualization and pupil assessment of the teachers' effectiveness. DAI, 42(7), 3097A.

194. Hull, J. A. (1976). Self-actualization of teachers, student estimate of teacher concern, and related other variables. DAI, 37(10), 6366A.

Self-Actualization

195. Hulsey, C. L. (1979). A comparison of relationships between reading ability and degree of self-actualization in prospective elementary and secondary teachers. DAI, 40(10), 5405A.

196. Jimmerson, R. M. (1977). The relationship between the adult educator's self-actualization and growth in community problem-solving groups. DAI, 38(11), 6468A.

197. Johnson, T. N. (1973). Effects of group test interpretation upon changes in self-concept and self-actualization of college students. DAI, 34(8), 4745A.

198. Jorgenson, R. D. (1968). Relationship of teacher perception to student and teacher self-actualization. DAI, 30(1), 134A.

199. Jury, L. E. (1973). teacher self-actualization and pupil control ideology. DAI, 34(8), 4631A.

200. Keahey, S. P. (1973). The relationship of self-actualization and adjustment in retirement and the implications for curriculum development in adult education. DAI, 34(7), 3814A.

201. Keeler, D. J. (1978). The treatment effects of a group guidance program on selected self-actualization characteristics of gifted secondary age students. DAI, 39(6), 3376A.

202. Keller, K. L. (1982). Burnout in baccalaureate nursing students as it relates to self-actualization and coping methods. DAI, 44(7), 2094.

203. Kempster, J. (1979). Teaching towards the self-actualization of the learning child with psychoneurological dysfunction: A psycho-orthopedagogical perspective. DAI, 41(2), 598A.

204. Kennard, M. A. (1983). A study of the relationship between teachers' perceptions of self-actualization needs and their perceptions of satisfaction with the teaching profession. DAI, 44(3), 630A.

205. Keyton, F. R. (1965). Some relationships between a measure of self-actualization and various aspects of intermediate grade teacher effectiveness. DAI, 26(8), 4450.

206. King, A. P. (1971). The self-concept and self-actualization of university faculty in relation to student perceptions of effective teaching. DAI, 32(7), 3615A.

207. Kiss, I. A. L. (1975). A comparison of self-actualization, adjustment, and sociometric status of high school students. DAI, 36(8), 5047A.

208. Knauf, J. W. (1974). A study of growth toward self-actualization in a family life education program. DAI, 35(9), 5927A.

209. Knight, L. W. (1973). Self-actualization: A study of ten people and how their perceptions provide a humanizing approach to education. DAI, 34(2), 558A.

210. Knott, J. E. (1975). An investigation of the relationship between self-actualization and subsequent academic achievement among college students. DAI, 37(2), 810A.

211. Kuehn, W. L. (1973). Self-actualization and engagement-involvement responses to literature among adolescents. DAI, 34(11), 6947A.

212. Kurtz, F. C. (1972). Nominations, self-report scores, and an empirical approach to college student self-actualization. DAI, 33(6), 2819A.

Self-Actualization

213. Labach, P. A. (1969). Self-actualization in college students: Interrelationships of self-actualization, personal characteristics, and attitudes in subcultures of liberal arts freshmen and seniors. DAI, 31(3), 1013A.

214. Lapham, A. G. (1984). Student self-actualization and leadership potential in three types of nursing programs (ADN, BN, RN-BSN). DAI, 45(7), 2005A.

215. Leatherwood, H. W. (1971). The effectiveness of small-group procedures in the classroom as aids in movement toward self-actualization in junior college students. DAI, 32(9), 4988A.

216. Lewis, M. B. (1976). A model program for a community college English department of assisting nursing home residents to achieve self-actualization through learning experiences. DAI, 37(6), 3449A.

217. Lloyd, J. T. (1977). Behavioral changes toward self-actualization as a function of vicarious pretraining. DAI, 39(2), 781A.

218. Mace, R. E. (1970). Factors influencing the decisions of teachers to become administrators: A study of the differences in self-actualization and job satisfaction occurring between future administrators and career teachers. DAI, 32(1), 132A.

219. MacLeod, M. I. (1973). The effects of a staff development program emphasizing self-study and introspection on teacher progress towards self-actualization. DAI, 34(3), 1036A.

220. Marshall, B. M. (1972). Elementary principals' primary bases of power and the relationships with the teachers' need fulfillment and self-actualization. DAI, 33(9), 4745A.

Self-Actualization

221. McCauley, V. M. (1977). Effects of school management systems upon the self-actualization of teachers and students. DAI, 38(7), 3854A.

222. McLaughlin, B. S. (1972). An assessment of teacher performance, attitudes and self-actualization as related to participation in Iota workshops. DAI, 33(2), 532A.

223. Mead, V. H. (1983). Ego identity status and self-actualization of college students. DAI, 44(9), 2707A.

224. Meyer, M. M. (1977). The relationship of the self-esteem of students to the self-actualization of teachers. DAI, 38(8), 4552A.

225. Miller, J. A. (1984). The relationship between prospective teachers' level of self-actualization and their attitudes toward handicapped persons. DAI, 45(6), 1718A.

226. Miller, R. R. (1972). A study of self-actualization in an introduction to education course. DAI, 33(5), 2223A.

227. Mitchell, C. E. W. (1974). Use of self-actualization scales as a predictor of academic success. DAI, 35(11), 7084A.

228. Moates, F. K. (1970). Some effects of human relations training on facilitative communication and self-actualization of resident assistants at the University of Georgia. DAI, 31(11), 5773A.

229. Murray, J. E. (1981). A content analysis of federally funded career education projects to determine the extent to which the content is favorable or unfavorable to indicators of self-actualization. DAI, 43(3), 653A.

230. Murray, M. E. (1968). Self-actualization and social values of teachers as related to students' perception of teachers. DAI, 30(3), 1026A.

Self-Actualization

231. Myers, J. R. (1977). Predicting public education administrator styles through administrator values, organization environmental factors, self-actualization levels, and specific demographic information. DAI, 38(2), 577A.

232. Natko, J. Growth toward self-actualization with inservice and pre-service teachers. DAI, 34(11), 7052A

233. Nemecek, F. D. (1972). A study of the effect of the human potential seminar on the self-actualization and academic achievement of college under-achievers. DAI, 32(12), 6766A.

234. Newlon, R. E. (1968). Relationship between self-actualization and educational achievement at the high school level. DAI, 29(5), 1453A.

235. Noll, R. L. (1976). Teacher self-actualization and pupil control ideology-behavior congruence. DAI, 37(11), 6882A.

236. O'Brien, A. M. (1974). Attitudes of adult students toward grades and grading as a function of level of self-actualization and GPA. DAII, 35(2), 826A.

237. O'Donnell, J. (1982). Effects of personal development courses on self-actualization. DAI, 43(2), 405A.

238. Oganowski, J. L. (1984). The relationship between burnout, somatic complaints and illnesses and levels of self-actualization of registered nurses in Columbus, Ohio. DAI, 45(3), 756A.

239. Okun, H. (1979). Self-actualization and its influence upon in-service achievement in the workshop setting. DAI, 40(9), 5012A.

240. Pappas, J. C. (1977). Changes in the dimensions of self-actualization as a result of participation in a personal growth class. DAI, 39(11), 5657B.

241. Paulk, L. J. (1972). A study of teacher self-actualization philosophical orientation and student attitudes. DAI, 33(4), 1378A.

242. Pelser, H. J. M. (1983). The role of electronics as an optional subject in the self-actualization of the secondary school pupil. DAI, 45(5), 1318A.

243. Preyar, C. F. (1973). A study of self-actualization and adaptive behavior of civil service employees in the Cincinnati public schools. DAI, 34(1), 6322A.

244. Pusateri, P. D. (1976). A study of the relationships between self-actualization and job satisfaction in teaching. DAI, 36(11), 7216A.

245. Quinn, J. G. (1974). Teacher self-actualization and high school student interest in Biology. DAI, 35(6), 3544A.

246. Render, G. F. (1973). The relationship between locus-of-control, self-concept, self-actualization and cognitive and affective outcomes of instruction. DAI, 34(8), 4886A.

247. Ridge, R. A. (1968). Self-actualization, achievement and other factors as a function of college students in selected housing settings. DAI, 30(1), 139A.

248. Roesch, I. H. (1975). Analyses of relationships between measures of self-actualization, discovery teaching climate, and selected characteristics of secondary science students in residential schools for the deaf. DAI, 36(7), 4408A.

249. Rosendahl, P. L. (1972). A study of the relationship between three helping conditions and self-actualization of adult learners. DAI, 33(4), 1405A.

250. Ross, M. C. (1983). An investigation of the relationship between selected characteristics of doctoral students, as an expression of self-actualization, and their choice of doctoral nursing program. DAI, 44(9), 2685A.

251. Ryan, M. M. (1974). An analysis of the differential effects of coeducational and single-sex schools on self-actualization and academic achievement. DAI, 35(5), 2698A.

252. Salva, D. M. (1968). Self-actualization and its relationship to intensity of vocational interests of male college freshmen. DAI, 30(2), 837B.

253. Sands, B. L. (1970). An exploratory study of self-actualization and self-perception of competency among Michigan family life teachers. DAI, 31(7), 3425A.

254. Schlesinger, L. B. (1978). Assessing student outcomes in psychological education: A validation study of measures of self-esteem, locus of control, self-actualization, and vocational maturity. DAI, 39(6), 3383A.

255. Schmeltz, W. G. (1982). Self-actualization and research activity among university professors. DAI, 43(2), 331A.

256. Schroeder, C. C. (1972). An analysis of the impact of residential setting on the development of selected dimensions of self-actualization. DAI, 33(8), 4188A.

257. Sheikh, A. H. H. (1985) Relationships between job satisfaction and self-actualization among teachers in the San Diego city schools (California). DAI, 46(7), 2449B.

258. Sheldon, D. K. (1981). The relationship between teacher self-actualization and length of teaching experience among elementary school teachers in a district experiencing enrollment decline. DAI, 42(2), 534A.

259. Sherman, L. L. (1969). Movers and perseverers in education: An investigation of interests, values, personality factors, self-actualization, need satisfaction and job satisfaction among movers into counseling and into administration and among perseverers in teaching. DAI, 31(3), 1023A.

260. Shull, J. L. (1981). The relationship of self-actualization and interpersonal behavior among school principals to teacher self-esteem and student achievement. DAI, 42(4), 1425A.

261. Silver, F. M. (1976). An empirical investigation of the relationship between teacher self-actualization and classroom openness. Unpublished doctoral dissertation, university of Ottawa, Canada.

262. Smith, M. L. H. (1968). The facilitation of student self-directed learning as perceived by teachers with high and low levels of self-actualization and dogmatism. DAI, 29(5), 1467A.

263. Stanley, G. E. (1980). The relationship between and change in career attitude maturity and self-actualization in students participating in a precollege academic program. DAI, 41(9), 3960A.

264. Sterchele, N. R. (1973). An investigation of some relationships between self-actualization and child-centeredness among teachers. DAI, 34(9), 5607A.

265. Sweeney, P. J. (1975). Could a humanistic high school English unit improve student self-actualization? DAI, 36(3), 1421A.

266. Thatcher, J. S. (1980). The interrelationship of leader self-actualization and life stressors to the resultant incidence of reported medical problems of middle management educators. DAI, 41(6), 2398A.

267. Tomblin, J. (1978). Self-actualization and group training: Relationship to ratings of teacher performance. DAI, 39(8), 4080B.

268. Tucker, F. C. (1970). A study of the relationships between: (1) teachers' levels of self-actualization and their teaching behavioral styles, and (2) teachers' teaching behavioral styles and the gratifications they derive from interacting with their students. DAI, 31(11), 5739A.

269. Wagman, J. R. (1979). The relationship of self-actualization of adult education faculty advisers to the to the self-actualization and program progress of their doctoral students. DAI, 40(10), 5287A.

270. Wanko, G. J. (1975). Level of self-actualization as it relates to expectations and perceptions of the college environment during the freshman year. DAI, 36(3), 1338A.

271. Ward, C. S. (1976). An investigation of differences between secondary special education and regular program teachers in terms of self-actualization theory. DAI, 37(3), 1420B.

272. Watson, H. W. (1972). The relationship between self-actualization and an individualized field centered under graduate teacher-education program. DAI, 33(5), 2229A.

273. Westerman, J. E. (1974). A comparison of the effects of a cooperative teacher education program with the effects of a conventional teacher education program on the degree of student-teacher self-actualization. DAI, 35(4), 2110A.

274. Wetzel, N. R. (1980). The relationship between organizational climate in elementary schools and self-actualization of certificated personnel. DAI, 41(9), 3832A.

275. White, R. K. (1973). The effect of a selected self-development program on participant self-actualization and academic achievement. DAI, 34(6), 3075A.

276. Wiley, R. C. (1974). Self-actualization of students participating in the junior block teacher education program at Oregon State University. DAI, 34(10), 6509A.

277. Wilkinson, J. M. 19173). The relation of two variations of classroom conditions, attitudes toward cheating, level of self-actualization, and certain demographic variables to the cheating behavior of college students. DAI, 34(9), 5671A.

278. Winecoff, F. W. (1973). The effect of an affective educational experience on the self-actualization of Oakton Community College students. DAI, 34(10), 6398A.

279. Wise, G. W. (1976). The relationship of sex-role perception and level of self-actualization in public school teachers. DAI, 37(9), 5674A.

280. Witchel, R. I. (1973). Effects of gestalt-awareness on self-actualization and personal assessment of student personnel graduate students. DAI, 34(8), 4766A.

281. Wolter, J. A. (1980). The relationship between administrative characteristics and self-actualization among high school administrators. DAI, 41(7), 2879A.

Self-Actualization

282. Zimmerman, K. W. (1970). verbal classroom interaction and characteristics including self-actualization of home economics teachers. DAI, 31(12), 7406B.

This section deals with human relationships that involve intimacy. The sources range from roommates to marriage. Self-actualization theory has contributed to our thinking and re-thinking about human relationships. New ideas about the meaning and development of love among human beings comes directly from self-actualization theory. The development of intimacy, concepts of mature love, the basis for and the reasons for maintaining marriage and childrearing all are effected by theories of self-actualization.

283. Diener, E. (1972). Maternal child-rearing attitudes as antecedents of self-actualization. Psychological Reports, 31(3), 694.

Attempted to discover parental attitudes of mothers which may have been related to self-actualization in their adult children. The significant results indicated a factor of "encouraging verbalizations" as related to self-actualization. Such concepts as "ignoring the child" and "avoidance of communication" were negatively correlated with self-actualization.

284. Farmer, R. (1982, Fall). Children's rights and self-actualization theory. Education, 103(1), 82-89.

States that children's rights have provoked increased debate and that the concept remains vague. The author presents an argument that Maslow's theory of self-actualization can provide a theoretical foundation for an understanding of children's rights.

285. Gelbond, B. (1979, Spring). Self-actualization and unselfish love. Journal of Religious Humanism, 13(2), 74-78.

Points out the fallibility of the idea that "selfishness" and "altruism" are opposites. The study indicates that "the process of regarding oneself highly, with a sense of active caring and affirmation, far from being a "selfish" turning away from others, allows a simultaneous opening of oneself toward others.

286. Gibb, L. L. (1968, January). Home background and self-actualization attainment. Journal of College Student Personnel, 9, 49-53.

Sought to associate home background variables with self-actualization. An instrument to measure self-actualization was correlated with a questionnaire designed by the author to assess background characteristics. The findings revealed that the educational level of parents, families of 1 to 3 children, working mothers and little or no formal religious training all were significant and positive in leading to self-actualization.

287. Hjelle, L. A. & Smith, G. (1975, June). Self-actualization and retrospective reports of parent-child relationships among college females. Psychological Reports, 36(3), 755-761.

Studied the self-report of college females on the attitudes of their parents and correlated them with a measure of self-actualization. High self-actualization was correlated with high perceived parental attitudes of acceptance, psychological autonomy, and lax control. Low self-actualizing subjects perceived parental attitudes as rejecting, psychologically controlling and firm control.

288. Insko, W. R. (1971, January). Developing family actualization: The Frankfort project. Family Coordinator, 20(1), 17-22.

Describes an experimental approach to developing family actualization based on workshops conducted in Frankfort, Kentucky.

The goals of the workshops were "personal growth, emphasizing the unfolding of individual capacities, and strengthening of interpersonal competence in family life" aimed at family self-actualization. The article reports favorable outcomes in both appreciation of the workshop by participants and in behavioral skills.

289. King, M. (1979, February). Parental self-actualization and children's self-concept. Psychological Reports, 44(1), 80-82.

Investigated the relationship between parental self-actualization and the self-concept of junior high age children. "Girls showed a stronger relationship to their parents than did boys; fathers had a greater influence on their children than did mothers, and the strongest sex combination was father-daughter. Few correlations were significant; all were low and accounted for small amounts of common variance."

290. Maslow, A. H. (1953). Love in healthy people. In A. Montagu (Ed.) The meaning of love. New York: Julian Press. Reprinted in M. DeMartino (Ed.) (1963). Sexual behavior and personality characteristics. Secaucus, New Jersey: Citadel Press.

Presents an overview of Maslow's understanding of love in self-actualizing people. Maslow discusses love and sexual relationships giving 11 characteristics of healthy love.

291. McIntire, W. G. & Nass, G. D. (1974). Self-actualizing qualities of low and high happiness in stable marriages. Research in the Sciences, 21, 1-10.

Studied 2 types of couples who were described as "satisfactorily" and "unsatisfactorily" married. The groups were divided into samples considered to be "stable-happy" and "stable-unhappy" couples marriage for 19 years. The results indicate that "stable-unhappy" couples were markedly lower on a measure of self-actualization.

292. Nystul, M. S. (1984, June). Positive parenting leads to self-actualization in children. Journal of Individual Psychology, 40(2), 177-183.

Argues first that the purpose of parenting is to help children toward self-actualization. The author provides the reader with examples of positive parenting at each of the levels of Maslow's hierarchy that hopefully will promote self-actualization.

293. Nystul, M. S. (1981, May). The effects of birth order and family size on self-actualization. Journal of Individual Psychology, 37(1), 107-112.

Investigated the effects of family size and birth order on self-actualization. The results indicate that a family size of 3 produces higher self-actualizers than other family sizes. The birth order effects indicate that an oldest male in a family of 3 is in the least advantageous position for self-actualization while the middle and youngest child in a family 3 are in the best position for self-actualization.

294. Olim, E. G. (1968, July). The self-actualizing person in the fully functioning family: A humanistic viewpoint. Family Coordinator, 17(3), 141-148.

Presents an analysis of several points of view regarding the family and rejects them in favor of a more humanistic view. The author describes the characteristics of self-actualization and applies these characteristics to the family.

295. Pascaretta, A. L. & Pino, C. J. (1981, November). Intimacy and self-actualization. Character Potential: A Record of Research, 9(4), 219-224.

Investigated the relationship between a measure of self-actualization and the Intimacy Potential Quotient (IPQ). A number of correlations were found to be significant and the authors provide a detailed description of each correlation along with detailed descriptions of each subscale of both the POI and the IPQ. A discussion of the implications of the results is provided.

269. Richards, A. C. (1972, Fall). Marriage vows to grow on. Colorado Journal of Educational Research, 12(1), 28-29.

Presents the author's personal marriage ceremony based on the influences of David Bakan, Erich Fromm, Sidney Jourard, C.G. Jung, and Abraham Maslow. The complete ceremony is included.

297. Simmons, S. & Ball, S. E. (1984, November). Marital adjustment and self-actualization in couples married before and after spinal cord injury. Journal of Marriage and The Family, 46(4), 943-945.

Assessed the relationship of self-actualization to marital adjustment before and after a serious spinal cord injury to the husband. "Both husbands and wives married after the injuries were significantly more inner-directed and had better marital adjustment than those married before the injuries."

298. Simon, J. (1982, Fall). Love: Addiction or road to self-realization, a second look. American Journal of Psychoanalysis, 42(3), 253-263.

Follows up a previous article (299) describing types of love or addictive relationships. Characteristics defining compulsive relationships are given. Characteristics such as sharing warmth, caring, affection and mutual growth as individuals are aspects of a constructive relationship.

299. Simon, J. (1975). Love: Addiction or road to self-realization? American Journal of Psychoanalysis, 35, 359-364.

Explores the idea that love can be an addiction which is defined as surrendering one's self to something obsessively and habitually. The author points out that most love relationships have parts of addiction and "mature love." The article concludes "when realized for its full potential, a love relationship greatly contributes to our growth and self-fulfillment as complete individuals." See also (298).

300. Tanzer, D. (1968, October). Natural childbirth: Pain or peak experience? Psychology Today, 2, 16-21, 69.

Presents a case for the psychological benefits of natural childbirth. The author's investigation reports the major finding to be that there are a number of psychological benefits. The article offers a number of anecdotal reports of both positive and negative experiences.

301. Travis, R. P. & Travis, P. Y. (1975, April). The pairing enrichment program: Actualizing the marriage. Family Coordinator, 24(2), 161-165.

Describes the Pairing Enrichment Program (PEP) and provides some evaluation data supporting its effectiveness. The authors conclude "in all the data to date, there has been a definite trend toward greater self and partner understanding, personal growth, interpersonal intimacy, warmth, appreciation, and development of the characteristics of the 'actualized' marriage."

302. Wills, B. S. (1974, Summer). The relationship between level of self-actualization and dissatisfaction with selected living arrangements. Journal of College and University Student Housing, 4(1), 15-18.

Study indicates that high self-actualizing males exhibit more dissatisfaction in residence hall living than low self-actualizing males because they preferred living arrangement that offered more opportunity for freedom and self-expression. Low self-actualizing males preferred living arrangement that were more structured and supportive. The data for females was confused relative to self-actualization but did indicate that females were overall more dissatisfied with their living arrangement.

303. Wise, G. W. & Strong, L. D. (1980, Fall). Self-actualization and willingness to participate in alternative marital and family forms. Adolescence, 15(59), 543-554.

Tested the hypothesis that high self-actualizers will be less likely to be willing to participate in traditional gender-differentiated marriage. This hypothesis received moderate support only from the female subjects. A second hypothesis was tested stating that high self-actualizers would be more likely to participate in a range of alternative marital and family forms. This hypothesis received conditional support from males.

Dissertations and Theses

304. Alley, P. M. (1982). Self-actualization and psychological androgyny in dual career families. DAI, 43(5), 1471A.

305. Anderson, W. T. (1981). Perceived health in the family of origin and levels of self-actualization. DAI, 42(2), 545A.

306. Bissett, D. W. (1983). Self-disclosure and self-actualization as predictors of love. DAI, 45(1), 400B.

307. Bochicchio, A. F. (1982). Relationship between self-actualization, love, gender, age, and duration of romantic relationship. DAI, 43(6), 1970B.

308. Caswell, L. G. (1982). Relationship of self-actualization and marital models to marital adjustment. DAI, 43(7), 2329B.

309. Dale, V. M. (1968). An exploration of the relationship of home managers' self-actualization to participation by family members in home activities. DAI, 30(2), 728B.

310. Darsa, S. D. (1976). Initiation of divorce as a function of locus-of-control, self-actualization and androgyny. DAI, 37(9), 4671B.

311. Dawson, F. (1969). An analytical study of the effects of maternal employment, of same-sex chum denial in preadolescence, and of residential mobility of self-actualization achievement in a sample of adolescents. DAI, 31(3), 925A.

312. Day, R. N. (1978). Effects of employment longevity, chronological age, and resident characteristics on self-actualization scores of houseparents for the institutionalized mentally retarded. DAI, 39(3), 1470A.

313. Desmonde, W. H. (1952). Self-actualization: Loving and strategic. Unpublished doctoral dissertation, Columbia University, New York.

314. Gregory Jr., J. F. (1983). The relationship between self-actualization and marital adjustment in intact families with teenage children in Catholic schools. DAI, 44(8), 2367A.

315. Hersch, L. E. (1976). The childless marriage: Sex-role identification and self-actualization as correlates of marital pattern. DAI, 39(11), 5559B.

316. Jayroe, K. E. (1979). Marital adjustment as a function of commitment and self-actualization. DAI, 40(2), 676A.

317. King, M. E. (1974). Parental self-actualization and child's self-concept. DAI, 35(1), 366B.

318. Lumpkin, W. C. (1981). The relationships of marital communication and marital adjustment with self-esteem and self-actualization. DAI, 42(6), 2883A.

319. Manning, K. J. (1983). Social pressure and self-actualization among lesbians and gay men in same gender marriages. DAI, 45(3), 1022B.

320. Neumann Jr., R. J. (1980). The relationship of marital status and quality to correlates of self-actualization among spinal cord injured men and their partners. DAI, 41(9), 3886A.

321. Nichols, D. L. (1980). Sex-role identity and its relationship to self-esteem, self-actualization and certain parental child rearing practices. DAI, 41(8), 3209B.

322. Noble, G. L. (1985). The characteristics of the actualized marriage: An exploratory study. DAI, 46(3), 655A

323. Price, A. H. (1976). Toward mature parenthood: Potential for growth through self-actualization and perceptual congruency. DAI, 37(6), 3090B.

324. Rudd, P. K. (1978). Psychological type, romanticism and self-actualization: Implications for mate selection and marital satisfaction. DAI, 39(12) 6140B.

325. Simmons, S. (1981). Marital adjustment and self-actualization among couples with spinal cord injured husbands: A comparison between pre- and post-marriage injury. DAI, 43(1), 80A.

Self-Actualization

326. Simpson, T. M. (1978). Intimacy level reciprocity in self-disclosure dyads and the relationship of disclosure level to self-actualization. DAI, 39(1), 1969B.

327. Slali, B. A. (1978). Marital success and self-actualization in husbands of professional women. DAI, 39(8), 4054B.

328. Songer, S. B. (1985). The relationships among marital satisfaction, components of marital satisfaction, and self-actualization in married men and women. DAI, 46(3), 949B.

329. Sriram, C. M. (1978). The relationship between self actualization and the levels of facilitative conditions in parent-adolescent communication. DAI, 39(7), 3492B.

330. Winstead-Fry, P. E. (1974). The relationship of self-actualization and articulation of body concept to the perception of dominance and to actual dominance in married couples. DAI, 35(10), 4966B.

331. Young IV, A. S. (1981). Self-actualization and marital adjustment in married dual-career couples. DAI, 42(5), 1969A.

This large section deals with the development and use of instruments for the measurement of self-actualization. Much of it centers around the Personal Orientation Inventory (POI) and the research on the validity, reliability and usefulness of this instrument. Other instruments have been developed for specific purposes. Also included in this section are many studies linking some measure of self-actualization to a number of other concepts, concerns, behaviors or theoretical positions.

332.   Abbott, R. D. & Harris, L. (1973). Social desirability and psychometric characteristics of the Personal Orientation Inventory. Educational and Psychological Measurement, 33, 427-432.

Purpose was to determine the relationship between the items and the scales of the POI on social desirability. The results indicate that the 2 major scales of the POI are confounded by a social desirability factor of about 28% for the Time Competence scale and about 10% on the Inner Directed scale.

333.   Anderson, H. N., Sison, G. & Wester, S. (1984, November). Intelligence and dissimulation on the Personal Orientation Inventory. Journal of Clinical Psychology, 40(6), 1394-1398.

Tested the hypothesis that high IQ subjects would be better at faking good scores on the POI than low IQ subjects. The hypothesis was rejected since both groups scored lower when attempting to fake good than control subjects supporting the general claim that the POI is resistant to faking.

334. Bonjean, C. M. & Vance, G. G. (1968). A short-form measure of self-actualization. Journal of Applied Behavioral Science, 4(3), 299-312.

Describes the background, purposes and design of a short-form structured, interview instrument for the measurement of self-actualization in organizations. The instrument is designed for use in organizations where time, expense and relative lack of skill in interviewing are important considerations.

335. Bonk, E. C., Knapp, R. R. & Michael, W. B. (1978, Summer). Personality growth among counselor trainees as measured by the Personal Orientation Dimensions. Educational and Psychological Measurement, 38(2), 519-521.

Designed to investigate changes in self-actualization among counseling master's degree students toward the end of their program. The POD scores revealed significant changes for 4 of the 13 scales in a positive direction toward self-actualization. The authors conclude that the study provides support for the construct validity of the POD.

336. Braun, J. R. (1966). Effects of "typical neurotic" and "after therapy" sets on Personal Orientation Inventory scores. Psychological Reports, 19, 1282.

Asked students in a social psychology class to respond to the POI as they thought "typical neurotics" would and again as they thought the same person would respond after two years of therapy. The scores were significantly different. The author concluded that since "S's were able to manipulate their scores so readily, the POI is highly transparent and should be used with caution in situations where persons may be motivated to make a good impression." See also (339).

337. Braun, J. R. & Asta, P. (1969, July). A comparison of "real" vs. "ideal" self with a self-actualization inventory. Journal of Psychology, 72, 159-164.

Investigated the ability to fake the POI. The results were mixed with 6 scales superior under the ideal instructions and 4 superior under the standard instructions.

338. Braun, J. R. & Asta, P. (1968). Intercorrelations between Personal Orientation Inventory and Gordon Personal Inventory scores. Psychological Reports, 23, 1197-1198.

Reports the intercorrelations between the POI and the GPI. The results are that 9 of the 48 correlations are significant with the GPI's Original Thinking scale most consistently related to POI dimensions. The authors conclude that this provides some support for Maslow's thinking that self-actualization and creativity are highly related.

339. Braun, J. R. & LaFaro, D. (1969, July). A further study of the fakability of the Personal Orientation Inventory. Journal of Clinical Psychology, 25(3), 296-299.

Tested 6 groups to verify an earlier study (336). The results of the earlier study were not supported. Four groups were tested under either standard instructions or fake good instructions. Further, 2 groups were given instruction in self-actualization. The authors conclude that "unless S's have special information about the POI and self-actualization, the inventory shows an unexpected resistance to faking."

340. Brooker, G. (1975). An instrument to measure consumer self-actualization. In M. J. Schlinger (Ed.) Advances in Consumer Research, Vol. 2. Chicago, Illinois: Association for Consumer Research.

Self-Actualization

Developed a personality measure based on Maslow's description of self-actualization specifically designed for market-related studies. The aim of the instrument was to measure consumer self-actualization. Reliability and validity are described and the results of the tests are presented.

341. Brown, E. C. & Smith, W. H. (1968). Measurement of existential mental health: Further exploration. Journal of Individual Psychology, 24, 71-73.

Attempted to determine if an instrument designed earlier (372) to measure mental health from an existential viewpoint would discriminate between groups of undergraduate students (ie, males and females, freshmen and seniors). The results indicate that women tend to have higher scores than men and senior tend to score higher than freshmen.

342. Coan, R. W. (1972). Review of the Personal Orientation Inventory. In O. K. Buros (Ed.), The seventh mental measurements yearbook. (pp. 121-123.) Highland Park, N.J.: Gryphon Press.

Provides a review of the POI as a suitable instrument for the measurement of self-actualization. The review provides some background on the concept of self-actualization, describes the major aspects of the POI and its theoretical assumptions and discusses some of the items. Overall, the review has only slight praise for the POI and concludes with the hope that better instruments will become available.

343. Damm, V. J. (1972, Summer). Overall measures of self-actualization derived from the Personal Orientation Inventory: A replication and refinement study. Educational and Psychological Measurement, 32(2), 485-489.

Replicates a previous study (344) in which scores on the Inner Directed scale or

69

combining the raw scores of the Time
Competence and Inner Directed scales provided
as good an overall measure of self-
actualization as the total score of the POI.
The purpose of this study was to report
intercorrelations among sub-scales of the POI
using a different population. The results of
this study were that the Inner Directed scale
or the Time Competence and Inner Directed
scales combined were the best predictors of
an overall measure of self-actualization.

344. Damm, V. J. (1969). Overall measures of
self-actualization derived from the Personal
Orientation Inventory. Educational and
Psychological Measurement, 29, 977-981.

Concludes that the Inner Directed scale or
the Inner Directed and Time Competence scales
combined provide the best indicator of
overall self-actualization as measured by the
POI. See (343) for a replication study.

345. Ecker, J. R. & Watkins, J. T. (1975, April).
Effects of response set and psychological
knowledge on answers to the Personal
Orientation Inventory. Journal of Clinical
Psychology, 31(2), 275-279.

Compared sophisticated with unsophisticated
subjects on change scores for the POI. The
authors report that this level of
sophistication should be taken into account
in any study which tests the ability to fake
of the POI since differences were obtained in
this study. Essentially, high knowledge
subjects tended to be able to raise their
scores while low knowledge subjects tended to
receive lower scores when trying to fake
good.

346. Fischer, J. & Knapp, R. R. (1977). The
validity of the Personal Orientation
Inventory for measuring the effects of
training for therapeutic practice.
Educational and Psychological Measurement,
37(4), 1069-1074.

Examined the relationship of scores on the POI to the facilitative conditions of empathy, genuineness and warmth. Overall, there were significant positive relationships between scores on the POI and the facilitative conditions.

347. Fisher, G. & Silverstein, A. B. (1969, April). Simulation of poor adjustment on a measure of self-actualization. Journal of Clinical Psychology, 25(2), 198-199.

Explored whether felons could fake bad on a measure of self-actualization. The results, using the POI, were that on 8 scales the fake bad scores were lower and on 1 scale they were higher than a control group. The authors conclude that felons recognize the social acceptability of the self-actualization concept but probably have a distorted view of it.

348. Forest, J. & Sicz, G. (1981, August). A review of the Personal Orientation Dimensions Inventory. Journal of Personality Assessment, 45(4), 433-435.

Reviews the development of the POD which is a refinement of the POI. The author gives background information on the new theorists incorporated into the new test, gives information regarding improvements and suggests continuing problems in the new test including test construction, theoretical justification and interpretation. The author also presents new problems including costs of scoring, failure new supporting research and problems of comparison with old research on the POI.

349. Forest, J. & Sicz, G. (1980, October). Data discrepancies in the Personal Orientation Inventory Manual. Journal of Personality Assessment, 44(5), 538-540.

Reports on data discrepancies in the Manual of the POI. The authors report some errors considered to be both minor and major. Some of these errors appear to be due to the number of questions left unanswered by subjects. However, some are unexplained.

350. Foulds, M. L. (1970). Effects of a personal growth group on a measure of self-actualization. Journal of Humanistic Psychology, 10(1), 33-38.

Reports that scores on the POI were significantly higher on 8 of 12 scales for persons who participated in a personal growth group than scores of the control group. The population consisted of "relatively healthy, growth-seeking college students.

351. Foulds, M. L. & Warehime, R. G. (1971, May). Effects of a "fake good" response set on a measure of self-actualization. Journal of Counseling Psychology, 18(3), 279-280.

Asked college students to try to fake good on the POI. The results indicate that rather than scoring higher on the POI fake good scores tended to be lower thus providing some evidence that the POI resist faking. The author indicates a caution that knowledge of the self-actualization model could help fake good scores.

352. Foulds, M. L. & Warehime, R. G. (1971, April). Relationship between repression-sensitization and a measure of self-actualization. Journal of Consulting and Clinical Psychology, 36(2), 257-259.

Compared scores on the Repression-Sensitization scale and the POI. The results indicate that college women tend to score higher on self-actualization than college males and that the relationship between scores on the R-S and the POI is negative and significant. The R-S is a measure using questions from the MMPI. Thus, high scores on the POI would compare to high scores on the R-S. Thus, the authors conclude self-actualizers use an approach defense strategy.

353. Fox, J., Knapp, R. R. & Michael, W. B. (1968). Assessment of self-actualization of psychiatric patients: Validity of the Personal Orientation Inventory. Educational and Psychological Measurement, 28(2), 565-569.

Compared hospitalized subjects with nominated non-self-actualizing, non-hospitalized and normal subjects in order to test the validity of the POI. The results contained some variability but "all POI scales significantly differentiated the hospitalized population from normal and self-actualized samples."

354. Goldman, J. A. & Olczak, P. V. (1981, Spring). Effect of test sensitization and knowledge about self-actualization on taking the Personal Orientation Inventory. Educational and Psychological Measurement, 41(1), 49-53.

Tested whether knowledge of self-actualization and, specifically, knowledge of the POI tended to increase subject's scores. This proved to be the case. The authors caution users of the POI to be sensitive to prior knowledge or of knowledge gained during therapy, for example, if POI scores are used to measure outcome.

355. Goldman, J. A. & Olczak, P. V. (1976, August). Effect of knowledge about self-actualization on faking the Personal Orientation Inventory. Journal of Consulting and Clinical Psychology, 44(4), 680.

Used a pre-test, post-test, control group design to study 3 conditions (fake bad, be honest again control and fake good) in testing the ability to fake of the POI of both knowledgeable and naive subjects. Pre-test scores were not significant. The results revealed that subjects not familiar with the POI were able to significantly lower their scores when asked to do so. Knowledgeable subjects can also lower their scores. Naive subjects, however, when asked to fake good were unable to do so. Knowledgeable subjects were able to raise their scores when asked to do so.

356. Goldman, J. A. & Olczak, P. V. (1975, April). Self-actualization and the act of volunteering: Further evidence for the construct validity of the Personal Orientation Inventory. Journal of Clinical Psychology, 31(2), 287-292.

Studied differences between volunteers and non-volunteers on a measure of self-actualization (the POI). It appears that volunteers score lower than non-volunteers supporting the hypothesis of the researchers that non-volunteers are more autonomous, thus more self-actualizing.

357. Graff, R. W., Bradshaw, H. E., Danish, S. J., Austin, B. A. & Altekruse, M. (1970). The POI: A validity check. Educational and Psychological Measurement, 30, 429-432.

Tested the validity of the POI using student ratings of dormitory assistants effectiveness as a criterion measure. The results indicated that Inner Directed, Self-Actualizing Value, Spontaneity and Acceptance of Aggression were primarily predictive of effectiveness in dormitory assistants. See also (86).

358. Gunn, Bruce. (1980, March). The self-actualizing case method. Journal of Business Education, 55(6), 250-255.

Presents a method for organizations to use in assessing potential managers and in promoting self-actualization in the participants. This article "presents a case procedure designed to assist trainees to "self-actualize" in perfecting their problem-solving skills. The rationale behind the SACM [self-actualizing case method] {brackets ours}; the role that the instructor, case leaders, and participants play in its execution; and the closed loop grading system used for peer evaluation are all intricate elements of this case procedure."

359. Hattie, J., Hancock, P. & Brereton, K. (1984, February). The relationship between two measures of self-actualization. Journal of Personality Assessment, 48(1), 17-25.

Compares the POD, a refinement of the POI, to the POI. The authors contend that there is little improvement in the POD and recommend that the POI be continued to be used rather than the POD.

360. Hix, J. A. & Hensley, J. H. (1978, July). Sensitivity of the POI to instructional set in military and college populations. Measurement and Evaluation in Guidance, 11(2), 117-122.

Studied "two independent participant status (military vs. civilian) X differential instructions (control vs. fake-high vs. fake-low) X sex of participant analyses of variance were conducted using scores from the TC [Time Competence] and I [Inner Directed] {emphasis ours} scales as the dependent variables." The results differ from a number of other studies in that this study revealed that naive subjects could fake-good. Participants could fake in either direction.

361. Hyman, R. B. (1979, October). Construct validity of Shostrom's Personal Orientation Inventory: A systematic summary. Measurement and Evaluation in Guidance, 12(3), 174-184.

Reviews many studies of the POI to determine construct validity. "The evidence ...lends considerable support to use of Id [Inner Directed] and Tc [Time Competence] {emphasis ours} scales as measures of two related but distinct aspects of self-actualization."

362. Ilardi, R. L. & May, W. T. (1968, Spring). A reliability study of Shostrom's Personal Orientation Inventory. Journal of Humanistic Psychology, 8(1), 68-72.

Provides test-retest, product-moment correlations for the scales of the POI. The authors report that while "by no means completely satisfactory from a psychometric point of view, the reliability findings of this study may be deemed encouraging ..."

363. Jansen, D. G., Knapp, R. R. & Knapp, L. (1976, Summer). Measurement of personality change in an alcoholic treatment program: Further validation of the Personal Orientation Dimensions. Educational and Psychological Measurement, 36(2), 505-507.

Designed to examine the validity of the POD as a measure of change in an alcohol treatment program in the direction of self-actualization. The conclusion of the study was that the alcohol treatment program was effective since 8 of the 13 POD dimensions were significant and positive in the direction of self-actualization.

364. Jansen, D. G., Knapp, R. R. & Michael, W. B. (1979, Summer). Construct validation of concepts of actualizing measured by the Personal Orientation Dimensions. Educational and Psychological Measurement, 39(2), 505-509.

Designed to replicate and extend an earlier study by Knapp and Comrey (369) comparing the Comrey Personality Scales (CPS) with the POI. This study compared the CPS with the POD. The findings were in essential agreement with the earlier study and the POD is significantly related to many scales of the CPS.

365. Jones, K. M. & Randolph, D. L. (1978, Spring). Construction and validation of a scale to measure Maslow's concept of self-actualization. Southern Journal of Educational Research, 12(2), 97-110.

Reports the development of an instrument to measure self-actualization as defined by Maslow. The authors report the content validity, reliability and "other positive characteristics" of a 9 factor instrument developed to measure self-actualization. Content validity was established by a panel of experts and reliability was established by the test-retest method.

366. Kay, E., Lyons, A. R., Newman, W. & Mankin, D. (1978). A test-retest study of the Personal Orientation Inventory. Journal of Humanistic Psychology, 18(2), 87-89.

Reports a test-retest reliability study of the POI. The results were mixed and the authors questioned the usefulness of a test-retest strategy for measuring the reliability of the POI for methodological concerns. This study did not find the high reliability coefficients found in some studies.

367. Klavetter, R. E. & Mogar, R. E. (1967). Stability and internal consistency of a measure of self-actualization. Psychological Reports, 21, 422-424.

Reports a study of the POI in which 3 scales (Inner Direction, Time Competence and Self-Actualization Value) accounted for almost all the variance. The authors conclude that performance on the POI could be more accurately and quickly gained by simply using these 3 scales.

368. Knapp, R. R. (1965). relationship of a measure of self-actualization to neuroticism and extraversion. Journal of Consulting Psychology, 29, 168-172.

Studied the relationship of the POI to the Eysenck Personality Inventory (EPI). Using the EPI, a high neurotic and low neurotic group was selected and mean scores obtained for each group. All mean differences were significant and the authors concluded that while the two instruments were developed from different theoretical perspectives, they both seem to tap a common mental health core.

369. Knapp, R. R. & Comrey, A. L. (1973, Summer). Further construct validation of a measure of self-actualization. Educational and Psychological Measurement, 33(2), 419-425.

Compared the POI with the Comrey Personality Scales (CPS). The study concluded that significant correlations were obtained. However, the authors maintain that "it is clear that the CPS and the POI as total instruments are measuring somewhat different aspects of the personality-value domain." See (364).

370. Knapp, R. R. & Fitzgerald, O. R. (1973, Winter). Comparative validity of the logically developed versus "purified" research scales for the Personal Orientation Inventory. Educational and Psychological Measurement, 33(4), 971-976.

Purpose of the study was to examine the "comparative usefulness for predicting change following encounter group experience of the original clinical (logically) developed POI scales as contrasted to "purified" research scales based on a synthesis of criterion-correlated and item factor analytic studies."

371. Knapp, R. R. & Knapp, L. (1978, Summer). Conceptual and statistical refinement and extension of the measurement of actualizing concurrent validity of the Personal Orientation Dimensions. Educational and Psychological Measurement, 38(2), 523-526.

Designed to compare the POI to the POD (a refinement of the original POI). The study revealed that there were acceptable correlations between several of the similar scales of the POI and the POD. The authors report that this presents evidence of the concurrent validity of the conceptually similar scales.

372. Kotchen, T. A. (1960). Existential mental health: An empirical approach. Journal of Individual Psychology, 16, 174-181.

Explored the relationship of the existential concept of meaning to mental health. Seven components were derived from existential psychology and philosophy and used to develop a questionaire to assess the agreement of 5 different groups on the order of the progression toward mental health. The author concludes that the study lends empirical validity to the existential conception of mental health. See (341) for a follow up study.

373. Leak, G. K. (1984, February). A multidimensional assessment of the validity of the Personal Orientation Inventory. Journal of Personality Assessment, 48(1), 37-41.

Indicates that the Inner Directed scale can serve as a measure of several key aspects of self-actualization but concludes that it is not a global measure of self-actualization since it fails to correlate with other self-actualization criteria. A table is presented containing correlations with many other criteria that might be construed to be associated, positively or negatively, with self-actualization. The authors constructed a face-validity instrument entitled the "Personal Reaction Inventory" (PRI) and after testing suggest that it would serve as well as the POI as a quick measure of self-actualization.

374. LeMay, M. L. & Damm, V. J. (1969, June). Relationship of the Personal Orientation Inventory to the Edwards Personal Preference Schedule. Psychological Reports, 24, 834.

Compared the POI with the Edwards Personal Preference Schedule. The results indicate that the two scales were not highly related and clear sex differences appeared in the study. The authors recommend that "such sex differences would be an important consideration for self-actualization theorists."

375. Martin, J. D., Blair, G. E., Rudolph, L. B. & Melman, B. S. (1981). Intercorrelations among scale scores of the Personal Orientation Inventory for nursing students. Psychological Reports, 48, 199-202.

Reported intercorrelations among the scales scores of the POI using nursing students as subjects. The scores from this sample were compared to those reported in the manual and were generally higher than those reported in the manual.

376. Martin, J. D. & Martin, E. M. (1977). The relationship of the Purpose In Life test (PIL) to the Personal Orientation inventory (POI), the Otis-Lennon Mental Ability test scores, and grade point averages of high school students. Educational and Psychological Measurement, 37(4), 1103-1105.

Appears that self-actualization and purpose in life as measured respectively by the POI and the PIL are highly correlated. The authors did not rule out the possibility that the relationship could have been based on secondary relationships with other variables not measured in this study.

377. Maslow, A. H. (1942). The dynamics of psychological security-insecurity. Character and Personality, 10, 331-344.

Presents the results of research using the Security-Insecurity test. The author provides the reader with methods, sampling techniques and the theoretical background of the test. See (378).

378. Maslow, A. H., Hirsh, E., Stein, M. & Honigmann, I. (1945). A clinically derived test for measuring psychological security-insecurity. Journal of General Psychology, 33, 21-41.

Provides definitions of psychological security and insecurity. The Security-Insecurity test was constructed using clinical observation and theoretical research in the concept of emotional or psychological security. This article presents the test itself, norms and cautions for use. See (377).

379. McClain, E. W. (1970, August). Further validation of the · Personal Orientation Inventory: Assessment of self-actualization of school counselors. Journal of Consulting and Clinical Psychology, 35(1, Pt. 1), 21-22.

Compared the ratings of level of self-actualization of guidance institute participants by 3 staff members who knew them best with scores on the POI. The correlations ranged from .23 to .69 and were significant in 11 of 14 measures. The results are interpreted by the author as evidence that the POI is a measure of self-actualization.

380. McKinney, F. (1967). The sentence completion blank in assessing student self-actualization. Personnel and Guidance Journal, 45(7), 709-713.

Used a sentence completion blank with categories such as frustration, conflict and personal identity scored by raters. Interrater reliability was established at .88 for classifications of self-actualizing, self-defeating and immobilizing-affective. Scores of college students were compared to scores of industrial supervisors and revealed significant differences. The author presents implications for counseling for the technique.

381. Murphy, T. J., DeWolfe, A. S. & Mozdzierz, G. J. (1984, Summer). Level of self-actualization among process and reactive schizophrenics, alcoholics, and normals: A construct validity study of the Personal Orientation inventory. Educational and Psychological Measurement, 44(2), 473-482.

Used an in-patient population to extend the

validity studies of the POI. The results indicate that the scores fell in the predicted pattern of most to least self-actualized scores for normals (medical patients), alcoholics, reactive schizophrenics and process schizophrenics. The findings were considered to be supportive of construct validity for the POI.

382. Noll, G. A. & Watkins, J. T. (1974, May). Differences between persons seeking encounter group experiences and others on the Personal Orientation Inventory. Journal of Counseling Psychology, 21(3), 206-209.

Differences between persons who sought encounter group experience and those that refused were explored. The differences discovered were attributed to the higher self-actualization scores of the females who sought the encounter group experience.

383. Oakland, J. A., Free, F., Lovekin, A., Davis Jr., J. P. & Camillerei, R. (1978, Spring). A critique of Shostrom's Personal Orientation Inventory. Journal of humanistic Psychology, 18(2), 75-85.

Provides an examination of the POI based on a review of the theoretical assumptions of the test, test construction, reliability and validity data and an overview of other research regarding the test. The article is critical of the attention paid to both empirical and theoretical concerns in the construction of the test. Overall, the authors insist that the test is badly in need of major revisions of both a theoretical and empirical nature.

384. Omizo, M. M., Rivera, E. & Michael, W. B. (1980, Summer). Self-actualization measures as predictors of ability in facilitative communication among counselor trainees. Educational and Psychological Measurement, 40(2), 451-456.

Compared POI scores with ability in

facilitative communication as measured by the Gross Rating of Facilitative Interpersonal Functioning Scale (GRFIF). The conclusion of the authors was that self-actualization measures show promise as predictors of the ability to act in facilitative ways for counseling trainees.

385. Paritzky, R. & Magoon, T. (1979, January). Human potential seminar outcomes as measured by the Personal Orientation Inventory and goal attainment inventories. Journal of Counseling Psychology, 26(1), 30-36.

Investigated the outcomes of a Human Potential Seminar, a structured group to psychological growth and learning. The goals of seminar are self-affirmation, self-determination, self-motivation and regard for others or, generally, self-actualization. The outcomes indicated that participants in the seminar were significantly higher in self-actualization and in the goals of the seminar than a control group. The goals of the seminar were measured by self-report and the authors point out the dangers of this method.

386. Prescott, M. R., Cavatta, J. C. & Rollins, K. D. (1977, December). The fakability of the Personality (sic) Orientation Inventory. Counselor Education and Supervision, 17(2), 116-120.

Investigated the ability of new counseling students to fake good on the POI even though they had received no instruction on self-actualization or the POI. The results indicated that positive, significant changes occurred on 4 of 12 scales and the authors conclude that incoming counseling students already have sufficient information to successfully fake good on the POI.

387. Price, G. E. (1976, Winter). Preliminary evidence regarding the validity of the Personal Orientation Inventory as a measure of the construct self-actualization. Educational and Psychological Measurement, 36(4), 1089-1092.

Compared pre- and post-test scores on the POI after a stressful events as measured by a polygraph, and two weeks later. The outcome was that there were significant differences on 2 of 12 subscales of the POI - Self Regard and Self Acceptance.

388. Raanan, S. L. (1973). Test review. Journal of Counseling Psychology, 20(5), 477-478.

Reviews the administration, scoring, reliability and validity of the POI. The author concludes that the POI "may provide an interesting focus for a therapeutic interview but would be of extremely limited value as either a diagnostic or research instrument. See (394) for a reply.

389. Reeves, T. G. & Shearer, R. A. (1973, February). Differences among campus groups on a measure of self-actualization. Psychological Reports, 32(1), 135-140.

Administered the POI to 5 groups of college students. The groups were identified as Blacks, white majority, white, overt, non-conformists, white, covert, non-conformists and white, non-affiliated. The POI scores were factor analyzed and 3 factors were obtained - self-actualization feelings, self-actualization thinking and self-concept. Black and white, majority students were significantly higher on self-actualization feelings and Black students were significantly higher on self-concept than white, non-affiliated students.

390. Ritter, K. Y. (1977, June). Growth groups and the Personal Orientation Inventory. Group and Organization Studies, 2(2), 234-241.

Criticizes the use of the POI as an outcome measure for personal growth groups. The author presents information regarding master's degree students in counseling at 3 different institutions and from 9 different personal growth groups. Finally, the author presents a rationale for why the POI should only be used in conjunction with other instruments, or not used at all, as an outcome measure.

391. Rofsky, M., Fox, J., Knapp, R. R. & Michael, W. B. (1977, Winter). Assessing the level of actualizing of psychiatric in-patients: Validity of the Personal Orientation Dimensions. Educational and Psychological Measurement, 37(4), 1075-1079.

Compared scores on the POD for hospitalized psychiatric patients and nominated normal and actualizing subjects. The results were in the predicted direction with hospitalized psychiatric patients scoring significantly lower on 12 of 13 POD scales than normal and actualizing subjects.

392. Rowe, W. (1973, October). The effect of "faking good" on the Personal Orientation Inventory. Measurement and Evaluation in Guidance, 6(3), 164-167.

Compared scores on the POI after two sets of instructions were given to subjects. The first set of instructions encouraged the subjects to try to look like a good potential teacher for their instructor. The second set involved trying to respond for a hiring personnel officer in a large-city, traditional school system. There were clear, statistical differences between the 2 groups with the first group scoring higher on the POI. The author hypothesized that students trying to please an instructor, who had presented himself as humanistic, would score higher than other students trying to present themselves as conventional.

393. Schatz, E. M. & Buckmastser, L. R.   (1984).
      Development of an instrument to measure self-
      actualizing   growth   in   preadolescents.
      Journal of Creative Behavior, 18(4), 263-272.

      Hypothesized that it was possible to assess
      self-actualization in children between 9 and
      12 years of age. The authors developed an
      instrument entitled the Reflections of Self
      by Youth (ROSY).   The study conducted
      suggests that self-actualizing growth of
      preadolescents is measureable and gives some
      further information on the relationship
      between self-actualization and creativity.

394. Shostrom, E. L. (1973). Comment on a test
      review: The Personal Orientation Inventory.
      Journal of Counseling Psychology, 20(5), 479-
      481.

      Responds to a test review (388) and presents
      research regarding the reliability and
      validity of the POI. The author concluded
      that the POI has been shown to be a "valuable
      diagnostic and research instrument as well as
      a useful therapeutic instrument."

395. Shostrom, E. L.   (1964). An inventory for
      the measurement of self-actualization.
      Educational and Psychological Measurement,
      24(2), 207-218.

      Describes the development of the POI. The
      author presents the scales, reliability,
      validity and items used in the POI as well as
      initial research conducted to measure the
      effectiveness of the POI as an instrument to
      assess self-actualization.

396. Shostrom, E. L. & Knapp, R. R. (1966). The
      relationship of a measure of self-
      actualization (POI) to a measure of pathology
      (MMPI) and to therapeutic growth. American
      Journal of Psychotherapy, 20, 193-202.

      Study involved giving the MMPI and the POI to
      two groups of subjects in therapy. Group 1
      was a beginning group and Group 2 was an

advanced group. The results show that as therapy progressed MMPI scores decreased and POI scores increased. The author conclude that the POI can be used as a measure of the outcome of therapy.

397. Shostrom, E. L., Knapp, R. R. & Knapp, L. (1976, Summer). Validation of the Personal Orientation Dimensions: An inventory for the dimensions of actualizing. Educational and Psychological Measurement, 36(2), 491-494.

Compared persons nominated as self-actualizing or non-self-actualizing with their scores on the POD. All scales significantly differentiated the two samples thus providing evidence of the validity of the POD.

398. Silverstein, A. B. & Fisher, G. (1973). Internal consistency of POI scales. Psychological Reports, 32, 33-34.

Used scores of 500 prisoners on the POI to determine internal consistency. The results showed only low to moderate internal consistency.

399. Silverstein, A. B. & Fisher, G. (1972). Item overlap and the "built-in" factor structure of the Personal Orientation Inventory. Psychological Reports, 31, 492-494.

Endeavored to determine the degree of item overlap contributing to factors in the POI. There is a built-in factor structure but that whether this structure is attributable to the item overlap itself or to relationships between latent variables of self-actualization that the POI was designed to measure was not determined by this study.

400. Silverstein, A. B. & Fisher, G. (1972, July). Cluster analysis of Personal Orientation Inventory items in a prison sample. Multivariate Behavioral Research, 9(3), 325-330.

Scores of prisoners on the POI were clustered to determine the relationship of the clusters to the original scales scores. While cluster scores and scale scores compared favorably, cluster scores were only fair predictors of scale scores.

401. Snyter, C. M. & Allik, J. P. (1981, October). The ability to fake of the Personal Orientation Dimensions: Evidence for a lie profile. Journal of Personality Assessment, 45(5), 533-538.

Resistance of the POD to deliberate faking was investigated. An analysis of the data concluded that the POD was resistant to faking good and the article provides some evidence of a "lie Profile" which distinguishes deliberate attempts at faking good.

402. Starrett, R. H. (1976). Modifications of the Personal Orientation Inventory for improved specific trait prediction. Journal of Consulting and Clinical Psychology, 44(4), 676-677.

Describes an attempt to improve the capacity of the POI to predict specific traits of self-actualization. The article provides information on a 6 step procedure aimed at modifying the POI. The article provides the reader with the modified scale form POI content identification, means, standard deviations, internal consistency coefficients and keying instructions.

403. Tosi, D. J. & Hoffman, S. (1972, Spring). A factor analysis of the Personal Orientation Inventory. Journal of Humanistic Psychology, 12(1), 86-92.

Factor analyzed the POI. The results determined 3 factors labeled Extraversion, Open-mindedness and Existential Non-Conformity. The authors indicated these factors were in line with other descriptions of healthy personality development. The authors further questioned the necessity of the number of scales of the POI.

404. Iosi, D. J. & Lindamood, C. A. (1975, June). The measurement of self-actualization: A critical review of the Personal Orientation Inventory. Journal of Personality Assessment, 39(3), 215-224.

Reviewed the reliability and validity of the POI as well as faking and social desirability aspects in light of research. The authors conclude that POI offers potential but should be considered a research instrument.

405. Ulies, M. J. & Shybut, J. (1971). Personal Orientation Inventory as a predictor of success in Peace Corps training. Journal of Applied Psychology, 55(5), 498-499.

Compared POI scores with final selection after Peace Corps training. The results indicate significant relationships with considerable sex differences for several scales.

406. Warehime, R. G. & Foulds, M. L. (1973, Winter). Social desirability response sets and a measure of self-actualization. Journal of Humanistic Psychology, 13(1), 89-95.

Compared scores on the POI with the Edwards Social Desirability Scale (EDSD) and the Marlowe-Crowne Social Desirability Scale (MCSD). The results were in the predicted direction with positive correlation with the EDSD and non-significant or negative correlations with the MCSD.

407. Weinrach, S. G. & Knapp, R. R. (1976, Summer). Level of school counselor actualizing and student perception of guidance services: Further validation of the Personal Orientation Inventory. Educational and Psychological Measurement, 36(2), 501-504.

Investigated level of counselor actualization

and student evaluations of the high school guidance program. The results were that the more actualizing the counselors the more likely the students were to assign high ratings to the guidance program.

408. Wills, B. S. (1974, May). Personality variables which discriminate between groups differing in level of self-actualization. Journal of Counseling Psychology, 21(3), 222-227.

Studied the relationship between self-actualization, self-concept, values and achievement motivation. The results indicate that personality dimensions do discriminate between males and females and that males and females differ significantly in level of actualization. It is also clear that different combinations of personality variables differentiated between males and females.

409. Wright, L. & Wyant, K. (1974, Winter). Factor Structure of self-actualization as measured from Shostrom's SAV scale. Educational and Psychological measurement, 34(4), 871-875.

Factor analyzed the Self-Actualizing Value scale of the POI. In general, the results supported Maslow's scheme of self-actualization since factors generated conformed to Maslow's theory.

Dissertations and Theses

410. Bartels, W. J. (1976). The effects of a western meditation on a measure of self-actualization. DAI, 37(9), 5596A.

Self-Actualization

411. Benson, E. B. (1975). A comparison of the characteristics of self-actualization as measured by the Personal Orientation Inventory and the Sixteen Personal Factor Inventory to quantitative levels of thirteen components of the blood. DAI, 37(2), 873A.

412. Bieniewski, A. M. (1972). The effects of a student-centered self-development course on self-actualization as measured by the Personal Orientation Inventory. DAI, 34(2), 576A.

413. Bullard II, T. (1976). Construction of an attitude scale based on Maslow's iterative definition of self-actualization and comparison to Shostrom's operationally defined measure -- the Personal Orientation Inventory. DAI, 37(9), 4721B.

414. Eller, W. C. (1980). The effect of adult enrichment courses on self-actualization as measured by Shostrom's POI. DAI, 42(2), 501A.

415. Fifield, M. R. (1973). The measurement of self-actualization. DAI, 34(4), 1745B.

416. Frankenberg, E. L. (1972). Self-actualization and environment: The Personal Orientation Inventory as a measure of personal growth among undergraduates in a living-learning community. DAI, 33(11), 6087A.

417. Gellerman, R. J. (1976). Positive and negative verbal phrases as a measure of self-actualization. DAI, 37(4), 1984A.

418. Jones, A. (1980). The development of a short measure of self-actualization. DAI, 42(5), 2028B.

419. Jones, K. M., Jr. (1975). The construction and validation of an instrument to measure self-actualization as defined by Abraham Maslow. DAI, 36(4), 2026A.

420. Owens, J. M. (1972). Personal Orientation Inventory real-ideal response set measures of self-actualization and congruency in an encounter-group and marathon-group. DAI, 33(10), 5498A.

421. Schrange, D. F. (1977). Use of the Personal Orientation Inventory, a measure of self-actualization, in the selection of resident advisors. DAI, 39(3), 1377A.

422. Shaffer, C. S. (1976). The ego-identity status interview as a predictor of positive change in self-actualization of university counseling center clients participating in human potential seminars. DAI, 37(10), 537B.

423. Tolliver, J. H. (1980). A description of the effect of values clarification on the self-actualization of a group of urban high school teachers as measured by Shostrom's Personal Orientation Inventory. DAI, 41(1), 213A.

Self-actualization theory has had an effect of the conduct of business, industry and management. The writing and research reported here focuses mainly on the hierarchy of needs as developed by Abraham Maslow. Other research and theory has focused upon the purposes, climate, productivity and job satisfaction of employees. This is another area in which it is necessary that more research and thinking be done. The relationship between individual self-actualization, corporate concerns and profit remain unclear, undefined and undeveloped. There is clearly room for new thinking, research and writing.

424. Baxter, G. D. & Bowers, J. K. (1985, August). Beyond self-actualization: The persuasion of Pygmalion. Training and Development Journal, 39(8), 69-71.

Argues that productivity of workers is based more on the meaning they see in their work than upon skill. The author uses the theory of Victor Frankl and criticizes Abraham Maslow's self-actualization theories of motivation and self-actualization and instead advocates Logotherapy as a management tool. The article provides 4 questions for managers to help them define meaning in work and 9 principles to help workers fine meaning in their work.

425. Betz, E. L. (1984). Two tests of Malsow's theory of need fulfillment. Journal of Vocational Behavior, 24, 204-220.

Reports a two part study of Maslow's theory of human motivation. Three occupational groups composed of women college graduates were used as subjects - professional-managerial, clerical-sales and homemakers. The findings of the study indicate that "homemakers appear to have less likelihood of need deficiency in the areas of security-safety and autonomy, but their esteem needs are less likely to be met than if they were to enter the work world outside the home.... Overall, the findings suggest that, at least for many women who are college graduates, opportunities for self-actualization play an important role in life satisfaction."

426. Brooker, G. (1976). The self-actualizing socially conscious consumer. Journal of Consumer Research, 3(2), 107-112.

Studied individuals who exhibited socially conscious consumer behavior. In general, the study concludes that socially conscious actions and self-actualization are related. In fact, the author found that demographic factors, which are often used in consumer research, were not as predictive as personality factors, such as self-actualization.

427. Bruce, G. D. & Bonjean, C. M. (1969, Summer). Self-actualization among retail sales personnel. Journal of Retailing, 45(2), 73-82

Conducted a study of self-actualization of employees in a large department store. The subjects were given a measure of self-actualization, interviewed and data were collected on wages, employee sales and supervisor's evaluation of the employee. Wages and supervisor evaluation were not significantly related to self-actualization. However, productivity emerged as most consistently related to self-actualization.

428. Cangemi, J. P. & Mitchell, D. W. (1975, May). A brief psychology of healthy and unhealthy organizations. Psychology, 12(2), 46-50.

Provides characteristics of unhealthy organizations, gives an overview of Maslow's assumptions regarding a self-actualizing organization and discusses organizational leadership. The article provides information and theory for consideration for managers.

429. Crookston, B. B. (1975, September). Human development: Actualizing people in actualizing organizations. Journal of College Student Personnel, 16(5), 368-375.

Argues for a concept of human development which has as a primary goal of higher educational self-actualization. The author compares different philosophies contending for dominance in higher education and examines the dangers of some of them.

430. Fruehling, R. T. (1976, October-November). Student self-realization and human relations training in the cooperative work experience curriculum. Technical Education News, 36(1), 2-4.

Advocates the goal of education as self-realization. The author argues that combining human relations training with technical training makes an ideal curriculum.

431. Goodman, R. A. (1968). On the operationality of the Maslow need hierarchy. British Journal of Industrial Relations, 6, 51-57.

Studied engineers and assembly line workers' job satisfaction using Maslow's hierarchy of needs as the basis for a questionnaire developed by the author. The findings showed no dominant motivation for engineers or assembly line workers. The implication, drawn by the author, is "that the work situation in and of itself adequately satisfies the security, social and ego needs such that the employees' preferences are no longer ordered." The author concludes that "a job which offers no real hazards, reasonable security, and a good level of interaction opportunity will serve to breakdown the hierarchical relationships posed by Maslow."

432. Hall, D. T. & Nougaim, K. E. (1968). An examination of Maslow's need hierarchy in an organization setting. Organizational Behavior and Human Performance, 3, 12-35.

Presented research aimed at testing Maslow's hierarchy of needs. The findings of the study involving the first 5 years of selected managers' careers provided no strong evidence for Maslow's hierarchy nor for a revised two-level hierarchy. However, the authors did report that as the managers advanced their needs for safety diminished and needs for affiliation, achievement, esteem and self-actualization increased. They attributed this to a model of sequential career stages.

433. Hamm, B. C. & Cundiff, E. W. (1969, November). Self-actualization and product perception. Journal of Marketing Research, 6, 470-472.

Tested housewives for level of self-actualization using a Q-sort technique that asked the subjects to rank cards with product names first as "like them" and second as "want to be." The difference was used as measure of congruence and divided into a high self-actualizing group and a low self-actualizing group. The results of the study report clear differences between products selected by high self-actualizing and low self-actualizing subjects as well as products picked as most like and least like in each group. The authors provide implications of the research for advertising and/or marketing managers.

434. Kumer, U. (1978, September). Self-actualization and organizational climate: A study of Indian managers. Indian Journal of Clinical Psychology, 5(2), 161-166.

Investigated the relationship between organizational climate and level of actualization of male, Indian managers. Generally, there appeared to be a negative relationship between an organizational climate of need achievement and self-actualization and a positive relationship between an organizational climate of need affiliation and self-actualization. The author concludes with a caution that climate variables may be difficult to interpret since Indian managers, in general, have a predisposition toward authoritarianism and security.

435. Lawler III, E. E. & Suttle, J. L. (1972). A causal correlational test of the need hierarchy concept. Organizational Behavior and Human Performance, 7, 265-287.

Studied Maslow's hierarchy of needs with two groups of managers. The groups were tested again after 6 months and 1 year to provide longitudinal data. The study provided no support of the Maslow's hierarchy of needs and the authors propose a two-level hierarchy to replace the multi-level hierarchy of Maslow.

436. Lessner, M. & Knapp, R. R. (1974, Summer). Self-actualization and entrepreneurial orientation among small business owners: A validation study of the POI. Educational and Psychological Measurement, 34(2), 455-460.

Hypothesized that merchandising-oriented entrepreneurs were more self-actualizing than craft-oriented entrepreneurs. Using the POI as a measure of self-actualization, the hypothesis was supported. The authors report 4 of 9 scales were statistically significant.

437. Maslow, A. H. (1969). Theory Z. Journal of Transpersonal Psychology, 1(2), 31-47.

Sets forth Maslow's ideas regarding management and organizations and differentiates between what Maslow labels as Theories X, Y and Z. Theory Z is a management orientation that leads to self-actualization. Maslow is speculative and theoretical in this article and labels his thinking pre-scientific rather than scientific in an attempt to differentiate between the kind of science that is aimed at discovery rather than verification. He maintains all principles set forth in the article are scientifically testable.

438. O'Reilly, A. P. (1973). The supervisor and his subordinates' self-actualization. Personnel Psychology, 26, 81-85.

Reports the results of a study of the effects supervisor's perception of subordinates skills and knowledge. The results indicate that the supervisors' were not knowledgeable of their subordinates' skills and knowledge and that this can play a powerful role in job satisfaction. The supervisor's role in the subordinate's perception, value of skills and opportunity to use them are positively related to job satisfaction and performance.

439. Pettit Jr., J. & Vaught, B. C. (1984, Summer). Self-actualization and interpersonal capability in organizations. Journal of Business Communication, 21(3), 33-40.

Assessed the level of self-actualization in first line and upper level managers in several organizations and compared level of self-actualization to ability to communicate in a supportive manner with subordinates. The results indicated a positive correlation between level of self-actualization and supportive communication skills.

440. Roberts, K. H., Walter, G. A. & Miles, R. E. (1971). A factor analytic study of job satisfaction items designed to measure Maslow need categories. Personnel Psychology, 24, 205-220.

Conducted a factor analytic study of responses of managers from 6 organizations to determine the extent to which factors empirically derived from the responses matched Maslow's hierarchy of needs. The results indicated mixed support for the usefulness of the hierarchy. The authors provide a discussion of the difficulty of this kind of research and suggest reasons for the outcome of the study.

441. Sullivan, D. R. (1972, June). Maslow's hierarchy of needs in relation to employment. Journal of Employment Counseling, 9(2), 94-95.

Offers Maslow's hierarchy of needs as a method of conceptualizing the practical needs of workers at different levels and the kind of aid they might require in satisfying their needs.

442. Wahba, M. A. & Birdwell, L. G. (1976). Maslow reconsidered: A review of research on the need hierarchy theory. Organizational Behavior and Human Performance, 15, 212-240.

Gives an overview of research regarding Maslow's needs hierarchy. Overall, the authors report that empirical research is mixed, at best, and tends to be non-supportive. The authors provide a discussion of the difficulties with testing the theory and the "conceptual, methodological, and measurement problems of the studies reviewed are detailed."

443. West, P. T. (1972, December). Self-actualization: Resolving the individual-organizational conflict. Clearing House, 47(4), 249-252.

Makes an argument for using the theories of organizational experts such as Herzberg, Maslow and McGregor to redesign educational administration to promote the self-actualization of teachers. The author offers suggestions for the reorganization of the educational institution that would better facilitate congruence between institutional goals and individual goals.

Self-Actualization

Dissertations and Theses

444. Dallinger, K. H. (1982). Self-actualization and employee turnover. DAI, 43(2), 548B.

445. Deming, A. L. (1977). A measure of self-actualization as a predictor of supervision effectiveness. DAI, 38(9), 5244A.

446. Jones, E. A. (1977). Self-actualization and its role in the organization: An exploratory study of the relationship between self-actualization, job performance and one's preception of the organization environment. DAI, 38(9), 5580A.

447. Ladenberger, M. E. (1971). An analysis of self-actualizing dimensions of top middle management personnel. DAI, 32(1), 605B.

448. Lessner, M. (1973). Self-actualization study of the small business entrepreneur. DAI, 34(4), 1727B.

449. Roberts, J. E. (1972). Self-actualization and the effectiveness of two patterns of supervision. DAI, 34(1), 300B.

450. Santavicca, G. (1984). Relationships between worker participation in work management and characteristics of healthy personality. DAI, 45(7), 2348B.

451. Thinnes, J. H. (1985). The relationship between personal variables and the self-actualization of management personnel. DAI, 46(3), 591A.

452. Vaught, B. C. (1979). An index of interpersonal communicative competence and its relationship to selected supervisory demographics, self-actualization and leader behavior in organizations. DAI, 40(12), 6351A.

Self-Actualization

453. Whitsett, D. A. (1967). Self-actualization and the modern formal organization. *DAI*, 28(6), 2616B.

454. Williams, R. A. (1984). Leadership styles and self-actualization: A study of executives. *DAI*, 45(5), 1615B.

455. Wilson, J. (1977). A study of the relationship between level of administrative position and self-actualization when analyzed by age, academic preparation and years of administrative experience. *DAI*, 39(1), 64A.

The connection between Western theories of
self-actualization and Eastern philosophical
and religious practices has not been lost on
researchers and writers. This section
explores the relationship of self-
actualization theory and a number of Eastern
practices. It appears that while languages
and cultures differ, the underlying
principles of human psychological health
have, at least partially, been discovered in
both.

456. Compton, W. C. (1984, June). Meditation and
self-actualization: A cautionary note on the
Sallis article. Psychologia: An
International Journal of Psychology in the
Orient, 27(2), 125-127.

Critiques a previous article. See Sallis
(462). The author argues that Sallis failed
to differentiate between different levels of
meditation practice. Thus, it is maintained
that the contradictions contained in the
original article if attention had been paid
to this variable.

457. Compton, W. C. & Becker, G. M. (1983,
November). Self-actualization and experience
with Zen meditation: Is a learning period
necessary for meditation? Journal of
Clinical Psychology, 39(6), 925-929.

Hypothesized that inconsistencies found in
research on the relationship between self-
actualization and Zen meditation could be
attributed to a learning period. The
research compared two groups. Group 1 were
practitioners of Soto Zen and group 2 were
undergraduates who had never meditated. The
results were in the hypothesized direction
with significant correlations on the Inner
Directed scale of the POI and partial support
from the Time Competence scale.

Self-Actualization

458. Ghaskadei, V. Y. (1981, July). Self-actualization and East-West synthesis. Indian Psychological Review/ Asian Journal of Psychology Education, 20(3), 40-41.

Reviews the work of Carl Rogers and Abraham Maslow .

459. Hjelle, L. A. (1974). Transcendental meditation and psychological health. Perceptual and Motor Skills, 39, 623-628.

Compared scores of experienced meditators with novice meditators on anxiety, locus of control and self-actualization. The result indicated that experienced meditators were significantly less anxious, more internally controlled and had higher levels of self-actualization than beginning meditators. The authors conclude that Transcendental Meditation has mental health and therapeutic implications.

460. Kline, K. S., Docherty, E. M. & Farley, F. H. (1982, January). Transcendental Meditation, self-actualization and global personality. Journal of General Psychology, 106(1), 3-8.

Compared two groups of recovering alcoholics and persons with general emotional problems one of which practiced Transcendental Meditation for 3 months and one of which did not. No significant differences in scores were apparent after the meditation. The authors discuss reasons for the lack of significance.

461. Kuppuswamy, B. (1976). Yoga and self-actualization. Manas, 23(2), 131-137.

Analyzes the works of such Western theorists as Carl Rogers, Gordon Allport, Carl Jung and Abraham Maslow as advocates of self-actualization and the relationship of theories of self-actualization to the teachings of Yoga. The Yoga Patanjali is used by the author to compare Eastern thought to self-actualization. The conclusion is that self-actualization as the goal of personality is "close to the methods and ideals" of Patanjalie in the Yoga Sutras.

462. Sallis, J. F. (1982, March). Meditation and self-actualization: A theoretical comparison. Psychologia: An International Journal of Psychology in the Orient, 25(1), 59-64.

Explored the theoretical foundations of Maslow's theory of self-actualization with the theoretical foundations of meditation. The author used 4 concepts from Maslow and compared them to the goals of meditation. The conclusion was that meditation and self-actualization are compatible and that meditation may be used to facilitate self-actualization. See (456) for a caution.

463. Seeman, W., Nidich, S. & Banta, T. (1972, May). Influence of Transcendental Meditation on a measure of self-actualization. Journal of Counseling Psychology, 19(3), 184-187.

Compared nonmeditators with subjects after 2 months of meditation. No significant differences were present in the pre-test and the post-test results showed that meditators were higher on 6 of 12 POI scales. The authors discuss the importance of the study and the implications for further research.

Dissertations and Theses

464. Bartels, W. J. (1976). The effects of a western meditation on a measure of self-actualization. DAI, 37(9), 5596A.

465. Bitting, A. L. (1976). Meditation and biofeedback: A comparison of effects on anxiety, self-actualization, openness and self-esteem. Unpublished doctoral dissertation. California School of Professional Psychology, Berkeley, California.

Self-Actualization

466. Burrows, C. H. (1984). The effects of meditation on counselor candidates' self-actualization. DAI, 45(3), 749A.

467. Dice Jr., M. L. (1979). The effectiveness of meditation on selected measures of self-actualization. DAI, 40(5), 2534A.

468. Geller, J. H. (1976). Ashram (Sikh) communities and self-actualization. DAI, 39(11), 5643B.

469. Joscelyn, L. A. (1978). The effects of the Transcendental Meditation technique on a measure of self-actualization. DAI, 39(8), 4104B.

470. Joseph, A. B. (1979). The influence of one form of Zen meditation on levels of anxiety and self-actualization. DAI, 40(3), 1335B.

471. Maher, M. F. (1978). Movement exploration and Zazen meditation: A comparison of two methods of personal-growth-group approaches on the self-actualization potential of counselor candidates. DAI, 39(9), 5329A.

472. Riddle, A. G. (1979). Effects of selected elements of meditation on self-actualization, locus of control, and trait anxiety. DAI, 40(7), 3419B.

473. Russie, R. E. (1975). The influence of Transcendental Meditation on positive mental health and self-actualization and the role of expectation, rigidity, and self-control in the achievement of these benefits. DAI, 36(11), 5816B.

474. Shapiro, J. S. (1975). The relationship of selected characteristics of Transcendental Meditation to measures of self-actualization, negative personality characteristics, and anxiety. DAI, 36(1), 137A.

475. Thorpe, T. J.   (1976).   The effects of integral Hatha Yoga on self-actualization, anxiety and body-cathexis in drug users. DAI, 37(5), 2551B.

476. Trausch, C. P. (1981). PSI training through meditation and self-actualization as related to PSI performance. DAI, 42(4), 1531A.

477. Truch, S. (1978). A study investigating the TM   technique,   self-actualization   and information processing. Unpublished doctoral dissertation. University of Calgary, Canada.

478. Weiner, D. E. (1976). The effects of Mantra Meditation and progressive relaxation on self-actualization, state and trait anxiety, and frontalis muscle tension. DAI, 37(8), 4174B.

Despite the attention minority affairs have received in recent years, this remains a neglected area of research in self-actualization theory. The self-actualization of non-dominate culture individuals is an area of study that is open and needed. Some questions that remain unanswered are: Is self-actualization a concept for the rich? Are there different patterns of self-actualization for members of different minority group members? Is socio-economic position more a factor than minority group membership? These questions and others involving gender, sexual preference and culture are crucial to our further understanding of the theory of self-actualization.

479. Feuerstein, R. & Hoffman, M. B. (1982, Winter). Intergenerational conflict of rights: Cultural imposition and self-realization. _Viewpoints in Teaching and Learning, 58_(1), 44-63.

Two basic rights are examined and explained - the right to be and the right to become. These basic rights are related to two human conditions - cultural imposition and self-realization. The authors explore the dominant manners of interaction between adults, children and culture and find them inadequate. They postulate another method of interaction labeled Mediated Learning Experience (MLE). The relationships and dimensions of this position are discussed.

480. Harper, F. D. & Hawkins, M. (1977, July). A profile of Black graduate students on the Personal Orientation Inventory. _Journal of Non-White Concerns, 5_(4), 168-174.

Investigated the profile of Black graduate students on the POI. Contrary to popular speculation, it appears that Black graduate students are more self-actualizing than traditional research has indicated. The authors argue that Black, lower socio-economic groups have been over-studied and generalizations drawn about an entire population. The authors suggest that there are differences that could be due to higher educational levels and higher socio-economic status.

481. Harper, F. D. (1974, Fall). Self-actualization and three black protesters. Journal of Afro-American Issues, 2(4), 303-319.

Studied 3 Black American protesters - Martin Luther King, Jr., Malcolm X and Frederick Douglass. The author sought to compare Maslows's 15 characteristics of self-actualization to these 3 Black Americans because only George Washington Carver and Frederick Douglass had been discussed previously as possible self-actualizers. The article examines the backgrounds of these 3 men to determine if any developmental factors could be discerned which would have contributed to their self-actualization.

482. Kirk, W. (1975, July). Where are you? Black mental health model. Journal of Non-White Concerns, 3(4), 177-188.

Presents an argument that a Black Psychology must be developed not based on traditional, White dominated psychological theory. The author presents a model of self-actualization based on Black experience. The goal is to de-emphasize the pre-occupation with prejudice, discrimination and racism and to emphasize knowledge of the Black experience by Blacks, their needs, and their humanity.

483. Knapp, R. R., Cardena, C. & Michael, W. B. (1978, Winter). Cross-cultural validation of the effects of dissimulation on a measure of actualizing. Educational and Psychological Measurement, 38(4), 1157-1163.

Investigated whether the Spanish language version of the POI could be faked good and whether results indicating the resistance of the POI to faking would be replicated in the Spanish language edition. The results of a study done in Nicaragua essentially duplicates research done in America.

484. Parham, T. A. & Helms, J. E. (1958, July). Relation of a racial identity attitudes to self-actualization and affective states of Black students. Journal of Counseling Psychology, 32(3), 431-440.

Studied the relationship of racial identity to self-actualization. The results indicate that "awakening black identity ... was positively related to self-actualization tendencies and negatively related to feelings of inferiority and anxiety."

485. Tate, G. A. (1972, Fall). Toward a Black psychology of the healthy personality. Colorado Journal of Educational Research, 12(1), 21-23.

Views the existing theories of self-actualization as "inaccurate conceptualizations, insofar as they fail to take into consideration, in more than a superficial sense, the experiences of the "counter cultures" of our society." The task of the author was to "re-mythologize" the concept of healthy personality in terms of the Black experience. A major focus of the Black experience, in the view of the author, is oppression. Encountering and confronting oppression becomes a major understanding of Black psychological health.

Dissertations and Theses

486. Church, A. T. (1985). Toward culture-relevant conceptions and assessment of healthy Filipino personality: An investigation, based on Filipino college

students, of the semantic and correlational structures of healthy personality. <u>DAI</u>, <u>46</u>(7), 2489B.

487. Davis, C. (1974). The analysis of self-concept and self-actualization manifestations by incarcerated and free black youth. <u>DAI</u>, <u>35</u>(11), 5636B.

488. Davis, M. L. (1980). Comparative study of changes in self-actualization between Black and White nursing students enrolled in predominantly White schools of nursing. <u>DAI</u>, <u>42</u>(8), 3191B.

489. Harper, F. D. (1970). Maslow's concept of self-actualization compared with personality characteristics of selected Black American protesters: Martin Luther King, Jr., Malcolm X and Frederick Douglass. <u>DAI</u>, <u>32</u>(1), 238A.

490. LaGarde, H. J. (1977). A systemic theory of self-actualization as applied to intercultural community programs in Louisiana. <u>DAI</u>, <u>38</u>(12), 6162B.

491. Logan, R. C. (1984). Self-concept and self-actualization among Black and White college students. <u>DAI</u>, <u>45</u>(5), 1345A.

492. Martin, A. C. (1976). Self-concept, self-actualization and occupational prestige aspirations of Black college students in the Virgin Islands. <u>DAI</u>, <u>37</u>(7), 4136A.

493. Yates, R. I. (1981). Counselor/educator self-actualization as a moderator of prejudice: Analogue study. <u>DAI</u>, <u>42</u>(2), 625A.

The history, understanding, and treatment of disorganized personality has naturally been a concern of self-actualization theorists. The opposite of self-actualization has attracted attention since any consideration of psychological health must concern itself with the removal of any pathological condition, at least theoretically. This section provides a background in such areas as depression, anxiety, substance abuse and criminal populations. The relationships between pathological behaviors and self-actualization remain cloudy and present the student of self-actualization an area of investigation that has many unanswered questions.

494. Berndt, D. J., Kaiser, C. F. & Van Aalst, F. (1982, January). Depression and self-actualization in gifted adolescents. Journal of Clinical Psychology, 38(1), 142-150.

Administered a depression inventory and a self-actualization instrument to academically gifted students to determine the relationship between self-actualization and depression. Both instruments were factor analyzed and the factors correlated. The results indicated low, positive correlations between high self-actualization and low depression. The high depressed/low self-actualized students were characterized by guilt, low self-esteem, learned helplessness and cognitive difficulty.

495. Cernovsky, Z. (1983, July). Dimensions of self-actualization and posttreatment alcohol use in fully and in partly recovered alcoholics. Journal of Clinical Psychology, 39(4), 628-632.

Contacted persons who had participated in an alcohol treatment program for a 1 year follow-up. The authors correlated scores on the POI with fully abstinent and drinking subjects. The results showed that abstinent persons were somewhat higher in self-esteem and freer in expression of feelings.

496. Dahl, R. & Jet, A. (1983). How the personality dimensions of neuroticism, extraversion and psychoticism relate to self-actualization. Personality and Individual Differences, 4(6), 683-685.

Studied the relationship between scores on the POI and the Eysenck Personality Questionnaire (EPQ). "The two major scales of the POI (Time Competence and Inner Directed), both separately and as a combined measure of self-actualization were correlated with the scores obtained on the EPQ. The results showed the hypothesized significant negative relationship between neuroticism and self-actualization and, for females only, the hypothesized significant positive relationship between extraversion and self-actualization. Contrary to hypothesis, no relationship between psychoticism and self-actualization was found."

497. deGrace, G. R. (1974, October). The compatibility of anxiety and actualization. Journal of Clinical Psychology, 30(4), 566-568.

Studied the relationship of anxiety to self-actualization. Most research and most theories view healthy persons as anxiety-free or low in anxiety. This study hypothesized, contrary to other research and theories, that anxiety was compatible with self-actualization. The study used junior college students as subjects and the major hypothesis, that there would be no difference in level of anxiety between high self-actualizing and low self-actualizing subjects, was confirmed. The author provides a discussion of the results in terms of traditional personality theories and previously reported research.

498. Dodez, O., Zelhart, P. F. & Markley, R. P. (1982, October). Compatibility of self-actualization and anxiety. Journal of Clinical Psychology, 38(4), 696-702.

Examined the empirical and conceptual relationship between self-actualization and anxiety. The authors administered the POI and two measures of anxiety to subjects. A content analysis of the POI revealed 33 items measuring anxiety were scored negatively. The removal of the anxiety items from the POI and rescoring the POI revealed scores that were positively related to anxiety. The authors conclude that the POI, as a measure of self-actualization, is biased against anxiety.

499. Doyle, J. A. (1976, December). Self-actualization, neuroticism, and extraversion revisited. Psychological Reports, 39(3, Pt. 2), 1081-1082.

Studied the relationship between the Eysenck Personality Inventory and the POI. The study reports modest relationships. Neuroticism is negatively correlated with self-actualization. Extraversion is positively correlated with self-actualization. The generally higher relationships in this study may be related to subjects' age.

500. Elizabeth, P. (1983, July). Comparison of a psychoanalytic and a client-centered group treatment model on measures of anxiety and self-actualization. Journal of Counseling Psychology, 30(3), 425-428.

Investigated outcomes of two different therapy groups. "Thirty volunteer graduate counseling students were randomly assigned by sex to one of four treatment groups involved in either a psychoanalytic or client-centered group treatment model.... Significant differences were found between treatment models in levels of group anxiety and in gains in self-actualization. The psychoanalytic groups reported higher anxiety, and the client-centered groups showed greater initial gains on the POI and maintained these gains at follow-up."

501. Fisher, G. (1968). Performance of psychopathic felons on a measure of self-actualization. Educational and Psychological Measurement, 28, 561-563.

Studied how psychopathic felons scored on the POI. The results indicate that their scores were below normals but higher than psychiatric patients.

502. Getsinger, S. H. (1976, August). Sociopathy, self-actualization, and time. Journal of Personality Assessment, 40(4), 398-402.

Compared male sociopaths and self-actualizers on measures of temporal behavior gained from estimation, projective and questionnaire techniques. The results show that the subjects differed significantly on half of the measures including time accuracy, delay, dominance, relatedness and evaluation of time models.

503. Ginn, R. O. (1974, January). Defensive and nondefensive repressors and sensitizers and self-actualization. Journal of Clinical Psychology, 30(1), 82-83.

Investigated the relationship between self-actualization, as measured by the POI, and nondefensive and defensive repressors and sensitizers, as measured by the Marlowe-Crowne Social Desirability (M-SCD) scale. The originally proposed repression-sensitization dimension seemed to leave no room for the psychologically healthy person. This study hypothesized that non-defensive repressors would show higher self-actualization than defensive repressors and that both repressors groups would be higher than sensitizers. Generally, the hypotheses were supported.

504. Jansen, D. G. (1974, July). Use of the Personal Orientation Inventory with state hospital alcoholics. Journal of Clinical Psychology, 30(3), 310-311.

Studied the usefulness of the POI in discriminating among a population of state hospital alcoholics. The author concludes that the POI may be of some usefulness as a rough screen of alcoholics from the general population but was of questionable value in discriminating in sub-groups of alcoholics.

505. Kilman, P. R. (1974, July). Self-actualization of female narcotic drug addicts. Journal of Clinical Psychology, 30(3), 308-310.

Investigated the scores of in-patient female drug addicts on the POI. The results presented a confusing picture of low scores on some scales and high scores on other scales. The author concludes that the result do show some indicates that a "here-and-now, feelings-oriented" therapeutic approach seemed recommended.

506. Maslow, A. H. (1965). Neurosis as a failure of personal growth. Humanitas, 3, 153-169.

Presents Maslow's argument that psychopathology occurs as a result need deficiency or of blocked gratification. The author argues for the replacement of a mental health/illness model with a more pragmatic and demonstrable concept of full or diminished humanness. The author indicates that psychopathology can occur for "conscious or unconscious" reasons, but for whatever the reason it can be conceptualized as a failure of self-actualization.

507. Mattocks, A. L. & Jew, C. C. (1974, Spring). Comparison of self-actualization levels and adjustment scores of incarcerated male felons. Educational and Psychological Measurement, 34(1), 69-74.

Correlated scores on the POI with a Q-sort Adjustment Scale. The subjects were male prisoners participating in group psychotherapy in a correctional psychiatric institution. Using the POI, high and low scores were compared to high and low adjusters. The results indicated that inmates who where high in POI scores also score significantly higher on adjustment.

508. McWilliams, J., Brown, C. C. & Minard, J. G. (1975, March). Field dependence and self-actualization in alcoholics. Journal of Studies on Alcohol, 36(3), 387-394.

Studied the effects of treatment programs on alcoholics. Both field-independence and self-actualization were significantly increased following a 6 week treatment program. However, no significant differences were obtained for the different forms of treatment drug-assisted individual, individual or mileau therapy.

509. O'Neill, M. F. (1976, September-October). Patients with hypertension: A study of manifest needs with self-actualization. Nursing Research, 25(5), 349-351.

Purpose of the study was to identify common psychological needs of patients with essential hypertension in order to provide appropriate nursing interventions. The POI and the Edwards Personal Preference Schedule (EPPS) were used to identify level of self-actualization and needs respectively. The results indicate that persons with hypertension have thwarted needs and lower levels of self-actualization. The nursing interventions are suggested but sketchy.

510. Osborne, J. W. & Steeves, L. (1981, December). Relation between self-actualization, neuroticism and extraversion. Perceptual and Motor Skills, 53(3), 996-998.

Studied the relationship of neuroticism and extraversion to self-actualization. In general, the results indicate that self-actualization is negatively related to neuroticism. However, contrary to other research, extraversion did not relate positively with self-actualization. The reasons for this departure are discussed.

511. Twemlow, S. W. & Bowen, W. T. (1977, April). Sociocultural predictors of self-actualization in EEG-biofeedback-treated alcoholics. Psychological Reports, 40(2), 591-598.

Attempted to predict factors which would lead to higher self-actualization scores for severely addicted in-patient alcoholics. Overall, pre-treatment scores were predicted by a background of white, well-educated persons from good homes and community support. After treatment scores were highly affected by "religiousness and religious affiliation."

512. Twemlow, S. W. & Bowen, W. T. (1976, Summer/Fall). EEG biofeedback induced self-actualization in alcoholics. Journal of Bio-feedback, 3(2), 20-25.

Studied the results of EEG biofeedback training for severely addicted male alcoholics. The findings show that the subjects tended to move in the direction of self-actualization on all but 2 scales of the POI but significantly only on the scales of Spontaneity and Freedom to Express Feelings.

513. Wilkins, W. E., Hjelle, L. A. & Thompson, M. (1977, October). Anxiety and actualization: A reconceptualization. Journal of Clinical Psychology, 33(4), 1001-1005.

Studied the relationship of self-actualization to anxiety. The result show that anxiety and self-actualization are negatively correlated.

Self-Actualization

514. Wilkins, W. E. & Krauss, H. H. (1978, October). Anxiety and actualization: Further research. Journal of Clinical Research, 34(4), 958-960.

Studied the relationship of self-actualization to anxiety, differentiating trait and state anxiety. The results show that high self-actualizers have lower trait anxiety and show state anxiety within the limits of their trait anxiety.

Dissertations and Theses

515. Jackson, M. L. (1980). Actualization of alcoholics anonymous members. DAI, 41(3), 1091B.

516. McElroy, D. M. (1976). A modified marathon with voluntarily institutionalized substance abusers: Effects on psychopathology, self-actualization and ward behavior. DAI, 36(11), 7213A.

517. Rocha, M. E. (1981). The effect of changed self-perception on vulnerability and self-actualization with military polydrug abusers. DAI, 42(6), 2581A.

The study of the peak experience can be one of the most exciting in the field of psychology. It is surprising that more has not been done. The field is difficult since it remains relatively undefined. Separating, classifying and defining this area of study is still not completed. The difference between peak experiences in the psychological sense and religious or mystical experiences in the religious sense has been investigated but the issue remains unsettled. The problem of who does and does not have peak experiences remains open. The idea of different types of peak experiences and the investigation of what promotes peak experiences is important. Finally, whether the artificial stimulation and purposeful teaching of techniques to create a peak experience is useful, of the same nature and ultimately worthwhile, is a badly needed area of research.

518. Armor, T. (1969). A note on the peak experience and a transpersonal psychology. Journal of Transpersonal Psychology, 1(1), 47-50.

Provides a challenge to practitioners of Transpersonal Psychology to develop methods of science to explore such "phenomena of a tacit and ineffable nature" as the peak experience. The article outlines issues that any student of the peak experience must resolve if the demands of science are to be met in Transpersonal Psychology.

519. Bertocci, P. A. (1965, October). On deeper dimensions. Contemporary Psychology, 10(10), 449-451.

Reviews A. H. Maslow's book Religions, Values and Peak Experiences. The reviewer provides a background for such works, suggests the importance of the book and gives criticisms of perceived shortcomings of the book.

520. Keutzer, C. S. (1978, Summer). Whatever turns you on: Triggers to transcendent experiences. Journal of Humanistic Psychology, 18(3), 77-80.

Investigated "triggers" or specific events which led to peak or transcendent experiences. The author compares her study with previous research published in 1974 of the general population with a sample of students. The student population and the general population differed mostly on religious triggers - with students reporting less.

521. Klavetter, R. E. & Mogar, R. E. (1967). Peak experiences: Investigation of their relationship to psychedelic therapy and self-actualization. Journal of Humanistic Psychology, 7(2), 171-177.

Reports the results of a study of "peakers" and "non-peakers" given the drug LSD as a part of therapy. The results indicate that "peakers" gained more from the experience and valued it more highly than "non-peakers" who described the experience negatively, devalued it and saw little benefit in self-enhancement.

522. Maslow, A. H. (1968, February). Music education and peak experiences. Music Educators Journal, 54, 72-75, 163-171.

Argues that the Arts must be an important part of the curriculum since music and sex are the two most frequently reported triggers of peak experiences and that peak experiences stimulate movement toward self-actualization. The author argues for music and the other Arts as a way to rescue the curriculum from the "value-neutral, goal-free meaninglessness into which it has fallen."

523. Maslow, A. H. (1962). Lessons from the peak experiences. Journal of Humanistic Psychology, 2, 9-18.

Provides an overview of the study of peak experiences, what is to be gained from them, some comparison with mystical experiences and the need of psychological science to study this phenomenon.

524. Maslow, A. H. (1961). Peak experiences as acute identity experiences, American Journal of Psychoanalysis, 21, 254-260.

Explores the place of the peak experience in identifying the unique identity of persons. The author provides 15 aspects of the peak experience which aid psychology in defining the concept of "identity." Maslow concludes the article with a discussion of the blending of Eastern thought on ego-transcendence and Western thought on self-actualization.

525. Maslow, A. H. (1959). Cognition of being in the peak experience. Journal of Genetic Psychology, 94, 43-66.

Argues that peak experiences are not uncommon and that there are identifiable "after-effects" which move the person toward self-actualization. Overall, this article emphasizes the importance of a cognitive aspect to peak experiences which leaves a lasting and changing truth with the experiencers.

526. Mathis, W. H. & McClain, E. W. (1968). Peak experiences of white and negro college students. Journal of Clinical Psychology, 24, 318-319.

Studied peak experiences between Blacks and Whites and between gender. The results report that overall females report more peak experiences than males and Whites report more peak experiences than Blacks.

527. McClain, E. W. & Andrews, H. B. (1969, January). Some personality correlates of peak experiences: A study in self-actualization. Journal of Clinical Psychology, 25(1), 36-38.

Hypothesized that more self-actualizing subjects would describe more peak experiences than less self-actualizing subjects. The results, using 3 different personality measures, supported the hypothesis.

528. Panzarella, R. (1980, Winter). The phenomenology of aesthetic peak experiences. Journal of Humanistic Psychology, 20(1), 69-85.

Content and factor analyzed descriptions of music and visual art peak experiences. Four phemenological factors were identified: renewal, motor-sensory, withdrawal and fusion-emotional. The article reports a complex system of associations and correlations as well as overall positive outcomes of the peak experience such as improved relationships, positive self feelings, boosted optimism and enhanced appreciation.

529. Ravizza, K. (1977, Fall). Peak experiences in sport. Journal of Humanistic Psychology, 17(4), 35-40.

Used the interview technique to ascertain personal experiences of athletes and to form a general characterization of athletes "greatest moment" in participation. The author describes common elements in athletes' descriptions of their "greatest moment" in sports and compares these to Maslow's descriptions of peak experiences.

530. Rowan, J. (1983, Spring). The real self and mystical experiences. Journal of Humanistic Psychology, 23(2), 9-27.

Introduces the concept that there is not one mystical experience but, rather, 7 which the author describes and references in the literature of mysticism. The author also argues for a "clean mysticism" and "a real religion with an aware psychology" that "offer a safe and sound basis for starting on the spiritual path."

531. Thorne, F. C. (1963). The clinical use of peak and nadir experiences reports. Journal of Clinical Psychology, 19, 248-250.

Collected peak and nadir experiences from subjects. These experiences were then used to create a classification system to encompass the great variety of experiences reported. The author suggests the importance of such experiences and their usefulness in understanding self-actualization.

532. Warmouth, A. (1963, Spring). The peak experience and the life history. Journal of Humanistic Psychology, 3(1), 86-90.

Argues that the worth of the peak experience for an individual cannot be properly understood unless it analyzed in the context of the total life history of the person.

533. Wuthnow, R. (1978, Summer). Peak experiences: Some empirical tests. Journal of Humanistic Psychology, 18(3), 59-75.

Randomly surveyed people who had and had not had peak experiences. The data indicate that most people have had peak experiences but that there is a clear tendency for some people to be more oriented toward peak experiences than others. The study also reports that there appear to be clear differences in values for peakers and non-peakers with the differences centered around material possessions versus social change/activism for peakers.

Dissertations and Theses

534. Leach, D. (1962). Meaning and correlates of peak experience. Unpublished doctoral dissertation, University of Florida, Gainesville, Florida.

535. Munkachy, L. D. (1974). Peak experiences and self-actualization in traditional and alternative styles of education: An exploratory study. DAI, 35(11), 7034A.

536. Noble, K. D. (1984). Psychological health and the experience of transcendence. DAI, 45(5), 1576B.

The area of politics and self-actualization is not one in which many references were found. It seems that it is an area which would attract more attention since the persons who enter politics have at their disposal vast resources which affect the lives of all of us. The psychological health of such persons would seem to be a major consideration for citizens. The development of methods for gaging such psychological health creates many research opportunities as well as the theoretical consideration of the ethical concerns of such research. The field is virtually unexplored in this area.

537. Anderson, W. (1975, Winter). The self-actualization of Richard M. Nixon. Journal of Humanistic Psychology, 15(1), 27-34.

Criticizes E. Shostrom's book Freedom to Be for its "inadequate" presentation of humanistic political science and, especially, for including Richard M. Nixon as an example of a self-actualizing person. See (540) for a rejoiner.

538. Carlson, J. M. & Hyde, M. S. (1980, September). Personality and political recruitment: Actualization or compensation. Journal of Psychology, 106(1), 117-120.

Sought to establish the relationship of self-esteem to political activists and office-seeking. The results show modest relationships with office-seekers low in need for esteem thus confirming what the author terms the actualization hypothesis.

539. Gunnison, H. (1967). Some hypotheses regarding psychological health and political-economic attitudes. Journal of Humanistic Psychology, 7, 10-17.

Attempted to examine the healthy view of existing political systems. The results indicate that psychologically healthy people tend not to be extremist, but tend to be left of center and favor a liberal political and economic set of values.

540. Shostrom, E. (1975, Winter). Rejoiner to Anderson's article. <u>Journal of Humanistic Psychology</u>, <u>15</u>(1), 35.

Responds to an article (537) criticizing his book <u>Freedom to Be</u>. Shostrom makes the point that his book was written before the problems of Watergate and that Nixon is still considered to be a major respected figure in international affairs despite the Watergate scandal.

541. Woolpert, S. (1982, Summer). A comparison of rational choice and self-actualization theories of politics. <u>Journal of Humanistic Psychology</u>, <u>22</u>(3), 55-67.

Provides an analysis of two political theories based on different theories of human nature. The author argues that the future depends very largely on which choice ultimately prevails.

Self-Actualization

Psychotherapy

The area of providing psychotherapy for individuals and groups has stimulated research, theory and practice aimed at understanding and developing optimal mental health in persons and in society. This section demonstrates the wide-ranging, fruitful, creative and compassionate ways in which self-actualization theory has stimulated work in this important area.

542. Cooper, G. L. (1971). T-group training and self-actualization. Psychological Reports, 28, 391-394.

Examined the impact of a T-group on trainees' self-actualization. The group members showed "significant change in the direction of becoming more independent and self-supporting, more flexible, more sensitive to their own needs and feelings, more spontaneous and more accepting of aggression."

543. Cooper, G. L. & Kobayashi, K. (1976, November). Changes in self-actualization as a result of sensitivity training in England and Japan. Small Group Behavior, 7(4), 387-395.

Compared results of sensitivity training T-groups conducted in England and Japan. The study revealed different outcomes and the authors caution that the application of the sensitivity training model should not be used in Japan unless "necessary cultural adaptions" are made.

544. Counseling Center Staff. (1972, May). Effects of three types of sensitivity groups on changes in measures of self-actualization. Journal of Counseling Psychology, 19(3), 253-254.

Compared changes in self-actualization in three different types of sensitivity groups with a control group. There was no difference in the control group and the three sensitivity training groups after the experience and no difference among groups in self-actualization.

545. Culbert, S. A., Clark, J. V. & Bobele, H. K. (1968). Measures of change toward self-actualization in two sensitivity training groups. Journal of Counseling Psychology, 15(1), 53-57.

Changes in self-actualization were measured in two sensitivity groups. One group showed overall changes toward self-actualization while the other group did not.

546. Deming, A. L. (1980, March). Self-actualization level as a predictor of practicum supervision effectiveness. Journal of Counseling Psychology, 27(2), 213-216.

Tested the hypothesis that level of self-actualization of counseling supervisors would have an effect on counselors in training. The hypothesis was rejected since overall counseling students tended to increase in level of self-actualization regardless of the level of self-actualization of their supervisor.

547. Dyer, W. (1978). Counseling for self-actualization: Helping clients eliminate their erroneous zones. Pupil Personnel Services Journal, 7(1), 17-32.

Paper based on a presentation made by the author in which he advocates that counselors be active agents of change as well as discusses many aspects of American life and education he feels are destructive.

548. Edwards, D. J. (1984, June). The effect on self-actualization of a personal growth programme based on co-counseling. South African Journal of Psychology, 14(2), 54-56.

Administered a measure of self-actualization to students participating in an intensive experiential program based on co-counseling or peer groups without using trained professionals. The results indicated that participants moved toward self-actualization and that the changes immediately after the experiences were still present at six months although not significantly different from the control group.

549. Elizabeth, P. (1983, July). Comparison of psychoanalytic and a client-centered group treatment model on measures of anxiety and self-actualization. Journal of Counseling Psychology, 30(3), 425-428.

Analyzed differences in outcomes from a psychoanalytic and a client-centered group on anxiety and self-actualization. The results indicate that the psychoanalytic group was higher in anxiety and client-centered group was higher in self-actualization immediately following the group and in a follow up 1 month later.

550. Follingstad, D. R., Kilmann, P. R. & Robinson, E. A. (1976, July). Prediction of self-actualization in male participants in a group conducted by female leaders. Journal of Clinical Psychology, 32(3), 706-712.

Sought to predict outcomes in self-actualization in males attending a growth group lead by women. The outcomes indicated that males who were lower in authoritarianism and agreed with feminist attitudes had higher self-actualization scores.

551. Foulds, M. L. (1971). Measured changes in self-actualization as a result of a growth group experience. Psychotherapy: Theory, Research and Practice, 8(4), 338-341.

Investigated the result of a weekly growth group of normal college students on self-actualization. The outcome showed that positive changes occurred in the direction of self-actualization. However, the author did not directly attribute these to the group experience itself.

552. Foulds, M. L. (1970, Spring). Effects of a personal growth group on a measure of self-actualization. Journal of Humanistic Psychology, 10(1), 33-38.

Designed to investigate the effects of a personal growth group self-actualization. The results showed that the experimental groups changed in positive directions toward self-actualization while the control group showed no changes in self-actualization scores.

553. Foulds, M. L. (1969). Positive mental health and facilitative genuineness during counseling. Personnel and Guidance Journal, 47, 762-766.

Undertaken to compare self-actualization scores with facilitative genuineness in counseling. The outcome showed a clear relationship between higher self-actualization scores and ability to communicate genuinely in counseling. The authors recommend more attention be paid to the personal development of counselors during training.

554. Foulds, M. L. (1969). Self-actualization and the communication of facilitative conditions during counseling. Journal of Counseling Psychology, 16(2), 132-136.

Investigated the relationship of level of self-actualization to the ability to communicate the facilitative conditions of empathy, genuineness and positive regard. The results indicate that ability to demonstrate empathy and genuineness are significantly associated with high self-actualization scores. See (588) and (599) for a replication.

555. Foulds, M. L. (1969, Spring). Self-actualization and level of counselor interpersonal functioning. Journal of Humanistic Psychology, 9(1), 07 92.

Studied the relationship of self-actualization to the counselor's level of interpersonal functioning. The outcome according to the author was that "particular positive personality characteristics of counselors appear to be significantly associated with their level of interpersonal functioning and their ability to provide the overall conditions of the 'therapeutic triad'."

556. Foulds, M. L. & Hannigan, P. S. (1977, May). Gestalt workshops and measured changes in self-actualization: Replication and refinement study. Journal of College Student Personnel, 18(3), 200-204.

Studied the effect of Gestalt therapy workshops on changes in self-actualization in an effort to correct some methodological flaws in some previous studies. The results were that increases in self-actualization scores were significant for participants in the workshops. See (557) and (558)

557. Foulds, M. L. & Hannigan, P. S. (1976, January). Effects of Gestalt marathon workshops on measured self-actualization: A replication and follow-up. Journal of Counseling Psychology, 23(1), 60-65.

Replicated a previous study investigating the effects of a 24 hour Gestalt marathon group on a measure of self-actualization. The results were significantly positive both for the immediate gains and for a 6-month follow-up. See (556) and (558).

558. Foulds, M. L. & Hannigan, P. S. (1976, Winter). Gestalt marathon group: Does it increase reported self-actualization? Psychotherapy: Theory, Research and Practice, 13(4), 378-383.

Studied the effect of a marathon group based on Gestalt therapy on the self-actualization of the participants. The outcome was an overall increase in self-actualization scores after the 24-hour group and, additionally, in the follow up 6 months later even greater increases. See (556) and (557).

559. Gilligan, J. F. (1974, February). Sensitivity training and self-actualization. Psychological Reports, 34(1), 319-325.

Administered a measure of self-actualization to 2 groups. Group 1 volunteered for a 24-hour sensitivity training program. Group 2 was a control group. The results were that "volunteers were found after training to be guided more by their own internal values, feelings and goals, and less controlled by external influences than were nonparticipants." These changes were still significant at a 6-week follow-up.

560. Glisson, C. A. (1973). Abraham Maslow's theory of self-actualization applied to the sensitivity training group. Group Psychotherapy and Psychodrama, 26(3-4), 77-87.

Outlines, in the author's opinion, the values and goals of sensitivity training. Further, the article presents the parallels of the values and goals of sensitivity training with Maslow's characteristics of self-actualization.

561. Hekmat, H. & Theiss, M. (1971, March). Self-actualization and modification of affective self-disclosure during a social conditioning interview. Journal of Counseling Psychology, 18(2), 101-105.

Compared high, moderate and low self-actualizing persons on level of self-disclosure. High self-actualizers had higher levels of self-disclosure before training based on conditioning principles and showed nonsignificant gains as a result of training.

However, the high self-actualizing group also showed resistance to extinction of self-disclosure after training.

562. Hershenson, D. B. (1982, March). A formulation of counseling based on the healthy personality. Personnel and Guidance Journal, 60(7), 406-409.

Combines the theories of Erikson and Maslow to develop a model of counseling. The author outlines 6 trends through the integration of these theories: survival, growth, communication, recognition, mastery, and understanding.

563. Johnson, S. & Johnson, N. (1979, September). Effects of various group approaches on self-actualization of graduate counseling students. Journal of Counseling Psychology, 26(5), 444-447.

Assigned subjects by sex to 2 different growth groups. Group 1 was a marathon group (2 8-hour sessions) and Group 2 was a combined group (1 8-hour session and 4 2-hour sessions). A measure of self-actualization was administered before and after the group experience and "some significant positive movement" toward self-actualization was noted. There was no significant difference between groups.

564. Jones, D. S. & Medvene, A. M. (1975, January). Self-actualization effects of a marathon growth group. Journal of Counseling Psychology, 22(1), 39-43.

Examined the effects of a marathon group on level of self-actualization and assessed the relationship between ego strength and changes in self-actualization. The results showed that "gains in self-actualization as a result of marathon group participation depended upon an individual level of ego strength upon entering the group."

565. Kilman, P. R., Follingstad, D. R., Price, M. G., Rowland, K. F. & Robinson, E. A. (1976, January). Effects of a marathon group on self-actualization and attitudes toward women. Journal of Clinical Psychology, 32(1), 154-157.

Investigated the impact of a marathon group on level of self-actualization and attitude toward women. The results were that both groups of female undergraduates moved in the direction of self-actualization. However, one group evidenced more profeminism before and had an even greater shift in that direction after the marathon group experience. The other group did not differ significantly from the control group either before or after the group experience.

566. Kilman, P. R., Sotile, W. M. and Fritz, K. R. (1978, December). Marathon versus weekly encounter-group treatment on self-actualization: Two years later. Group and Organization Studies, 3(4), 483-488.

Compared marathon and weekly encounter-group experiences effects on level of self-actualization. The results indicate no significant differences between the groups.

567. Kimball, R. & Gelso, C. J. (1974, January). Self-actualization in a marathon growth group: Do the strong get stronger? Journal of Counseling Psychology, 21(1), 38-42.

Outcomes of a weekend marathon were assessed using a measure of self-actualization. In general, the results pointed to an increase in self-actualization. The author reports that level of ego strength was unrelated to gains in self-actualization. Finally, the author discusses the conditions necessary for groups to be effective.

568. Kirkpatrick, J. S. (1979). A Maslovian counseling model. Personnel and Guidance Journal, 57, 386-390.

Self-Actualization

Uses Maslow's hierarchy of needs as a basis for creating goals for individuals and programs of counseling. The author proposes 14 categories of client concerns and suggestions for their use. The author identifies uses for the model in diagnosis, evaluation, counselor preparation and research.

569. Knapp, R. R. & Shostrom, E. L. (1976). POI outcomes in studies of growth groups: A selected review. Group and Organization Studies, 1(2), 187-202.

Summarizes and integrates a number of studies using the POI to assess outcomes of group experiences. The conclusion of the authors is that there evidence that the POI consistently identifies significant positive change toward self-actualization for participants of growth group experiences.

570. Langelier, R. (1982). Self-actualization and the therapeutic triad: A comparison between beginning and advanced counseling students. Psychology: A Quarterly Journal of Human Behavior, 19(2/3), 5-12.

Rated beginning and advanced counseling students on ability to communicate the therapeutic triad (empathy, genuineness and positive regard) and level of self-actualization. The results showed no significant relationship between level of self-actualization and effective communication of the therapeutic triad. There was no significant difference between beginning and advanced students on self-actualization and both groups were not highly self-actualizing.

571. Lavoie, D. (1974-1975). The phenomenological transformation of the self-concept towards self-actualization through sensitivity training laboratory. Philippine Journal of Psychology, 7-8, 3-12.

Designed to investigate hypothesized changes

toward self-actualization as a result of participation in sensitivity training. The hypotheses were that changes toward self-actualization would occur in a weekend encounter group, that these changes would be greater than a simple live together experience and that older persons would change more than a younger group. The results showed that changes toward self-actualization did occur and that the changes were greater for the weekend sensitivity group than for the live together experience. Contrary to expectations the older group showed less change than the other groups.

572. Lavoie, D. (1971-1972). The phenomenological transformation of the self-concept towards self-actualization through sensitivity training laboratory (Philippines). Interpersonal Development, 2(4), 201-212.

Reprint of (571) above.

573. Lombardo, J. P. & Fantasia, S. C. (1976, October). The relationship of self-disclosure to personality, adjustment, and self-actualization. Journal of Clinical Psychology, 32(4), 765-769.

Tested the hypothesis that high self-disclosure correlated with high self-actualization. The hypothesis was confirmed.

574. Macklin, T. J. & Rossiter, C. M. (1976, Fall). Interpersonal communication and self-actualization. Communication Quarterly, 24(4), 45-50.

Compared scores on the Interpersonal Communication Report (ICR) and the POI. The ICR measures expressiveness, self-disclosure and understanding. The ICR and the POI were positively and significantly correlated. The author concludes that 3 important communication variables have been identified and their relationship with self-actualization suggested.

Self-Actualization

575. Margulies, N. (1973, Fall). The effects of an organization sensitivity training program on a measure of self-actualization. <u>Studies in Personnel Psychology</u>, 5(2), 67-74.

Measured the effect of a T-group experience extended over a 4-month period with middle managers on self-actualization. "Results seem to indicate that there were important changes in the direction of increased self-actualization of participants in groups where application of T-Group learning was a significant part of the program design."

576. McIntire, W. G. (1973, November). The impact of T-group experience on level of self-actualization. <u>Small Group Behavior</u>, 4(4), 459-465.

Investigated the effect of T-group experience on level of self-actualization. The data indicate and the author concludes that T-group experience does have a positive effect on development of self-actualization. It is also indicated that the changes are maintained over time.

577. Meltzer, H. (1980, February). The impact of encounter groups: Actualizing differences between a T-lab group and a humanistic psychology group. <u>Small Group Behavior</u>, 11(1), 23-33.

Compared a T-group with a humanistic psychology course group. The article describes these two approaches, describes the group leaders' experience and background and describes the conduct of each group. The results are discussed and reasons for outcomes are suggested.

578. Omizo, M. M., Rivera, E. & Michael, W. B. (1980, Summer). Self-actualization measures as predictors of ability in facilitative communication among counselor trainees. <u>Educational and Psychological Measurement</u>, 40(2), 451-456.

Examined the predictive validity of the POI to identify ability to communicate the facilitative conditions in counseling. The Gross Rating of Facilitative Interpersonal Functioning Scale (GRFIF) was used to measure facilitative ability. The authors conclude that self-actualization measures show promise as predictors of facilitative ability.

579. Osborne, J. W. & Steeves, L. (1982, September). Counseling practicum as a facilitator of self-actualization. Alberta Journal of Educational Research, 28(3), 248-256.

Studied the effect of a counseling practicum on self-actualization. Overall, the study revealed that counseling practicum seems to have a profound effect on the self-actualization of the practicum students when compared to counseling students without practicum and non-counseling students with counseling practicum students evidencing higher levels of self-actualization.

580. Payne, T. J. (1981). Counselors' levels of self-actualization and prognoses for their clients: Further support for the POI. Journal of Drug Education, 11(4), 369-375.

Examined the usefulness of the POI as a screening device for drug counselors. Two groups of counselors were identified using the POI as high actualizing and low actualizing. These groups were then paired with clients and prognostic ratings given clients. The results were that high actualizing counselors' prognoses were significantly related on 2 scales while low actualizing counselors' prognoses were not related on any scales.

581. Peretti, P. O. & Stuart, H. S. (1981, September-October). Toward client self-actualization through insight-oriented group psychotherapeutic processes. ACTA Psychiatrica Belgica, 81(5), 444-451.

Conducted a study to identify variables associated with client self-actualization in group psychotherapy. The outcome was the identification of 6 most frequently perceived variables: information, reality testing, life-adjustment, self-awareness, autonomy and self-acceptance.

582. Perkins, R. J. & Kemmerling, R. G. (1983, January). Effect of paraprofessional-led assertiveness training on levels of assertiveness and self-actualization. Journal of College Student Personnel, 24(1), 61-66.

Discusses the effect of assertiveness training led by paraprofessionals on self-actualization of the participants. The authors report 2 conclusions of the study. First, there is significant and positive change in the assertiveness of the participants. Second, the groups resulted in increased self-actualization of the participants. The implications of these 2 conclusions are discussed in the article.

583. Reddy, W. B. (1973, November). The impact of sensitivity training on self-actualization: A one-year follow-up. Small Group Behavior, 4(4), 407-413.

Investigated the impact of sensitivity training on self-actualization and the maintenance of these effects over time. The results were that changes in self-actualization did occur after sensitivity group experience and these changes were maintained over at least 1 year.

584. Reddy, W. B. (1972, April). On affection, group composition, and self-actualization in sensitivity training. Journal of Consulting and Clinical Psychology, 38(2), 211-214.

Pre-selected interdenominational missionaries on compatibility for affection. Groups were composed of compatible and incompatible persons and it was hypothesized that incompatible persons would have greater gains on self-actualization after a sensitivity training experience. This hypothesis was supported and the author discusses the implications of preselected group in the article.

585. Reddy, W. B. (1972, March-April). Interpersonal compatibility and self-actualization in sensitivity training. Journal of Applied Behavioral Science, 8(2), 237-240.

Studied the effect of the dimensions from the FIRO-B (inclusion, control and affection) on changes in self-actualization in sensitivity training groups. The outcome was that different effects occurred for groups characterized as higher in inclusion, control or affection with affection seeming to give greater changes in self-actualization. The author discusses the results and makes recommendations in the article.

586. Reddy, W. B. & Beers, T. (1977, November). Sensitivity training ... and the healthy become self-actualized. Small Group Behavior, 8(4), 525-531.

Hypothesized that psychologically healthy persons would benefit more from sensitivity groups and show greater movement toward self-actualization than participants who viewed themselves as less healthy. The authors used the Tennessee Self-Concept Scale as a measure of self-actualization and confirmed the hypothesis.

587. Rosendahl, P. L. (1973, May). Effectiveness of empathy, nonpossessive warmth, and genuineness of self-actualization of nursing students. Nursing Research, 22(3), 253-257.

Tested whether a relationship characterized by empathy, genuineness and warmth would have an effect on self-actualization. The results indicate that there is a positive change in inner direction on the POI.

588. Rowe, W. & Winborn, B. B.   (1973, Spring).
     Self-actualization   and   counselor
     interpersonal functioning: A replication.
     Journal of Humanistic Psychology, 13(2), 79-
     84.

     Replicates an earlier study (554) by Foulds
     in which the facilitative conditions of
     empathy, genuineness and positive regard were
     found to be associated with level of self-
     actualization. This replication does not
     support the earlier findings.   The
     contradictory results are discussed by the
     authors. See (599).

589. Sargent, S. S. (1982, Winter). Therapy and
     self-actualization in the later years via
     nontraditional approaches.   Psychotherapy:
     Theory, Research and Practice, 19(4), 522-
     531.

     Indicates that a substantial minority of
     older citizens have mental health concerns.
     This article outlines many different
     approaches to helping with recommendations
     for the private practitioner.

590. Selfridge, F. F. & Vander Kolk, C.   (1976,
     March).   Correlates of counselor self-
     actualization   and   client-perceived
     facilitativeness.   Counselor Education and
     Supervision, 15(3), 189-194.

     Rated the ability of counselors to facilitate
     core conditions of empathy, congruence,
     positive regard and trust to level of self-
     actualization. The authors report a strong
     relationship between counselor effectiveness,
     as rated by clients, and self-actualization
     of the counselor.

591. Shostrom, E. L. (1973, Spring).   From
     abnormality to actualization. Psychotherapy:
     Theory, Research and Practice, 10(1), 36-40.

     Presents a model of therapy based on the
     concept of self-actualization.

592. Stewart, R. A. (1974). Self-realization as the basis of psychotherapy: A look at two eastern-based practices, Transcendental Meditation and alpha brain wave biofeedback. Social Behavior and Personality, 2(2), 191-200.

Examines Transcendental Meditation and biofeedback as contributers to other forms of psychotherapy to the promotion of individual self-actualization.

593. Thames, T. B. & Hill, C. E. (1980, September). The relationship of counselor self-actualization to counselor facilitativeness. Counselor Education and Supervision, 20(1), 45-49.

Studied counselors' level of self-actualization and self- and client perceived encouragement in a counseling session. Overall, it did not appear that counselors who viewed themselves as more self-actualizing did not view themselves as more encouraging and were not viewed by clients as more encouraging than counselors who viewed themselves as less self-actualizing. The instruments used in this study were the POI and the Barrett-Lennard Relationship Inventory.

594. Trotter, A. B., Uhlig, G. E. & Kennedy, C. (1979, Summer). Self actualization of male and female rehabilitation counselor students. Journal of Instructional Psychology, 6(3), 9-13.

Compared self-actualization of male and female rehabilitation counselors to determine if one gender revealed higher levels. The results failed to yield any differences. The authors discuss reasons for this result.

595. Trotter, A. B., Uhlig, G. E. & Fargo, G. E. (1971, September). Self-Actualization as a predictor of rehabilitation counselor success. Rehabilitation Counseling Bulletin, 15(1), 58-67.

Sought to "determine the degree of relationship between rehabilitation counselor success or effectiveness and (a) experience as a rehabilitation counselor and (b) degree of self-actualization." The authors used the POI as a research instrument determined that a combination of scales had some usefulness as predictors of counselor success.

596. Walton, D. R. (1973, November). Effects of personal growth groups on self-actualization and creative personality. Journal of College Student Personnel, 14(6), 490-494.

Reported that students involved in experiential growth groups demonstrated higher gains in self-actualization scores than students provided teaching about self-actualization.

597. Ware, J. R. & Barr, J. E. (1977, February). Effects of a a nine-week structured and unstructured group experience on measures of self-concept and self-actualization. Small Group Behavior, 8(1), 93-100.

Studied the effect of experiential growth groups on self-actualization using 2 different approaches to groups - structured and unstructured. Both groups reported higher levels of self-actualization after the group experience and there were differences between groups. The article includes a discussion of reasons for differences between groups.

598. Watkins, J. T., Noll, G. A. & Breed, G. R. (1975, August). Changes toward self-actualization. Small Group Behavior, 6(3), 272-281.

Reported 2 different studies. Study 1 compared brief to marathon group experiences on effect on self-actualization. Three groups of varying lengths ranging from 20 hours to 12 to 4. All groups reported change toward self-actualization with no significant difference between groups. Study 2 compared distributed versus massed exposure to group encounter. Three groups each consisting of 12 hours varying in time distribution were involved in group encounter. The results indicate that all groups gained in self-actualization with no significant difference among groups.

599. Winborn, B. B. & Rowe, W. (1972, January). Self-actualization and the communication of facilitative conditions - a replication. Journal of Counseling Psychology, 19(1), 26-29.

Replicated an earlier study (554) correlating the facilitative conditions of empathy, genuineness and positive regard to counselor self-actualization. The replication did not support such a relationship. The authors discuss the importance of replication in counseling research. See (588).

Dissertations and Theses

600. Aubry, W. E. (1970). An analysis of a one-week workshop for developing self-actualization and effective interpersonal behavior. DAI, 31(9), 4446A.

601. Barnett, L. C. F. (1971). The effect of silent communications upon counseling processes: An experimental study. The relevance of nonverbal behavior and self-actualization for counselor empathy and genuineness and client self-exploration. DAI, 31(12), 6336A.

602. Barrick, G. A. (1979). The effects of sensory awareness training on self-actualization in a personal growth group. DAI, 41(9), 3625B.

144

603. Bellanti, J. (1971). The effects of an encounter group experience on empathy, respect, congruence, and self-actualization. DAI, 32(11), 6668B.

604. Berger, A. O. (1979). The relationship of self-actualization of counselor-trainee to effectiveness in a practicum. DAI, 40(11), 5727A.

605. Billik, B. H. (1978). A study of the impact of a counseling practicum and initial self-actualization on the ability to demonstrate facilitative counseling behavior. DAI, 39(5), 2748A.

606. Bird, D. T. M. (1973). The relationship of self-actualization levels of counseled and non-counseled parents to perceptions of behavioral characteristics. DAI, 33(12), 6722A.

607. Bopp, J. T. (1977). The effect of structure and unstructured groups in various time modes on the self-actualization of undergraduate college students. DAI, 38(6), 3281A.

608. Brekke, D. M. (1978). Relationships among level of self-actualization, reflection of feeling skill, and counselor functioning. DAI, 39(6), 3363A.

609. Brittain, J. L. (1975). The relationship between perceived empathic understanding and self-actualization. DAI, 36(6), 3025B.

610. Broussard, J. K. (1982). Self-actualization measures as correlates of ability in facilitative communication of counselor trainees. DAI, 43(8), 2553A.

611. Brown, B. M. (1975). The effects of consciousness-raising group participation on stereotypic interests, behaviors, self-perceptions and self-actualization. DAI, 37(1), 518B.

612. Brown, R. W. (1974). A counseling practicum training program: The relationship between self-actualization and counseling skill. DAI, 35(12), 7643A.

613. Bryan, E. L. (1983). The effect of gestalt awareness exercises on measured self-actualization. DAI, 44(4), 987A.

614. Caffee, C. E. (1975). Bibliotherapy: Its effects on self-concept and self-actualization. DAI, 36(8), 5304A.

615. Cain, A. O. (1972). The relationship between growth in self-actualization and the numbers of perceived and mutually perceived relationships in sensitivity training groups. DAI, 33(5), 2232A.

616. Calhoun, T. W. (1982). The effects of indirect suggestion on self-actualization. DAI, 43(9), 2889A.

617. Campbell, R. E. (1975). The relationship of Arica Training to self-actualization and interpersonal behavior. DAI, 36(3), 1401B.

618. Cavatta, J. C. (1979). The effects of dissimulation on a measure of self-actualization among counselor trainees. DAI, 40(2), 809A.

619. Chance, G. R. (1981). The effects of group psychotherapy on the self-actualization of male inmates in a federal penitentiary. DAI, 42(6), 2499A.

620. Chitwood, T. M. (1976). The effect of centering on the self-actualization of master's level practicum counselors. DAI, 37(6), 3413A.

621. Cromwell, D. (1981). Therapists' responses to confrontation: An analogue study comparing theoretical orientation, level of self-actualization and experience level. DAI, 42(6), 2522B.

Self-Actualization

622. Darling, J. G. (1984). The relationship between the level of counselor self-actualization and faculty perception of the guidance program. DAI, 15(12), 3547A.

623. DeRocquigny, R. J. (1978). The effects of self-actualization on self-disclosure. DAI, 38(11), 5562B.

624. Elbert, W. E. (1969). Changes in self-concept, self-actualization, and interpersonal relations as a result of video feedback in sensitivity training. DAI, 30(12), 5233A.

625. Elizabeth, P. (1979). The effects of differential group treatments on the self-actualization of counselors in training. DAI, 40(6), 3115A.

626. Elliott, A. L. (1969). Fostering self-actualization of high school students through general semantics training in encounter groups. DAI, 39(9), 3632A.

627. Faillace, J. J. (1976). A measure of self-actualization as a predictor of counselor effectiveness with coached clients. DAI, 37(9), 5600A.

628. Farley, J. M. (1979). Leadership variables and self-actualization of participants in short-term counseling groups. DAI, 40(11), 5390B.

629. Field, E. S. (1979). Transactional analysis as a means toward development of self-actualization in individuals. DAI, 40(11), 5403B.

630. Findley, J. R. (1973). The relative effectiveness of rational encounter and basic encounter-groups in facilitating changes in self-actualization, self-perception, and interpersonal sensitivity. DAI, 35(1), 502B.

147

631. Flaherty Jr., R. W. (1974). The effect of muscular relaxation training upon the self-actualization of encounter-group participants. DAI, 35(3), 1443A.

632. Foulds, M. L. (1967). An investigation of the relationship between therapeutic conditions offered and a measure of self-actualization. DAI, 29(1), 120A.

633. Fulton, E. E. (1975). Self-actualization values and attitudes toward risk-taking behaviors following small group discussions. DAI, 36(12), 7884A.

634. Gadsden, C. (1981). Self-actualization and cohesiveness of college students in marathon or spaced short session groups. DAI, 42(5), 1960A.

635. Gammel, J. B. (1973). A study of the effects of levels of self-actualization on communication in small structured experiential groups. DAI, 34(8), 4740A.

636. Gardner, M. A. (1985). The relationship between self-actualization and the release of beta-endorphins in stressful situations. DAI, 46(4), 1373B.

637. Griesmer, R. (1975). A study of the changes in self-actualization and interpersonal distance in a sample of drug addicts actively enrolled in a drug rehabilitation program. DAI, 36(8), 4156B.

638. Grisham, J. H. (1972). A study of the effect of encounter type group experiences on the level of communication-discrimination skills and self-actualization of graduate counseling practicum students. DAI, 33(11), 6174A.

639. Groeneveld, L. C. (1969). The positive experience group encounter and its effect upon self-actualization. DAI, 30(9), 3726A.

640. Hall, J. C. (1974). Self-actualization, self-concept, respondent variables, and adjustment to Navy life. DAI, 34(7), 3465B.

641. Hannigan, P. S. (1975). An investigation of the comparative effects of a 16-hour and a 24-hour marathon gestalt workshop on a measure of self-actualization. DAI, 36(10), 6471A.

642. Hanson, J. J. (1984). The effect of EMG assisted alpha-theta training on the self-concept and self-actualization of counselor-trainees. DAI, 45(8), 2396A.

643. Hayes III, P. L. (1971). A study of the relationship of a measure of self-actualization to resident counselor effectiveness. DAI, 32(8), 4349A.

644. Hines, R. F. (1973). An investigation of self-actualization and helping experience in relation to provision of facilitative conditions in helping relationships. DAI, 34(9), 5628A.

645. Hood, W. D. (1968). Counselor-client similarity of self-actualization level and its effect on counseling outcome. DAI, 29(11), 3831A.

646. Horowitz, R. S. (1975). An investigation of the relationship between an intensive small-group experience and changes in interpersonal attitudes, behavior, and self-actualization. DAI, 38(9). 4462B.

647. Hull, D. (1971). The effect of laboratory training on self-concept and self-actualization. DAI, 33(1), 440B.

648. Hungerman, P. W. (1985). The effectiveness of the relaxation response in reducing anxiety and promoting self-actualization in counselor trainees. DAI, 46(4), 1324B.

649. Ibanez, P. (1984). The effects of the gestalt oriented group approach on the development of self-actualization in an adolescent population. DAI, 45(1), 375B.

650. Isaacson, E. B. (1982). The relationship of job satisfaction, attitude toward education and self-actualization with academic achievement among paraprofessional workers in the substance abuse field. DAI, 43(8), 2517A.

651. Ivers, J. J. (1978)1 The effect of counseling intervention and academic experience on the vocational maturity, job satisfaction and self-actualization of adult female participants in a federal upward mobility system. DAI, 39(4), 2064A.

652. Ivins, R. G. (1974). An exploration of the relationship between anxiety and self-actualization during initial counseling experiences. DAI, 35(5), 2685A.

653. Jones, D. S. (1972). Self-actualization effects of marathon growth group experience. DAI, 34(2), 855B.

654. Jones, G. S. D. (1980). The effects of the human potential seminar on the self-actualization and interpersonal relationship behaviors of undergraduate students. DAI, 42(7), 3074A.

655. Jones, J. P. (1981). Some changes in client levels of meaning-in-life and self-actualization in successful psychotherapy. DAI, 42(1), 375B.

656. Kyle, J. K. (1975). Effects of the EPI-C model upon self-actualization of clients in group counseling. DAI, 36(8), 5049A.

657. Langelier, R. (1975). The psychology of self-actualization involving the communication of therapeutic counseling skills between beginning and experienced counselors. DAI, 36(9), 4693B.

658. Lathey, R. K. (1971). A comparison of change toward self-actualization in marathon group counseling and traditional group counselinq. DAI, 32(7), 3692A.

659. LePage, H. L. (1974). Group process and outcome: A study of interaction patterns and changes in self-actualization among three marathon encounter groups varying in levels of self-actualization. DAI, 35(8), 5027A.

660. Levene, R. I. (1980). The effects of microcounseling-personal growth groups and microcounseling only on the self-actualization of community college students. DAI, 41(6), 2455A.

661. Liddle, H. A. (1974). Effects of a microlab experience upon college students' interpersonal behavior and movement toward self-actualization. DAI, 35(4), 1982A.

662. Liggitt, D. H. (1974). The relationship of micro-counseling, self-actualization, and teacher verbal responses. DAI, 35(8), 5028A.

663. Lynn, A. W. (1972). Measures of self-actualization changes and their relationship to interaction preferences among encounter group participants. DAI, 33(4), 1443A.

664. Marburg, G. S. (1980). The role of brief, individual, directive and nondirective psychotherapy in facilitating self-actualization among clients who have demonstrated an internal or external locus of control. DAI, 41(8), 3187B.

665. Marinaccio, M. M. R. (1976). An investigation of effects of the human potential seminar on the self-actualization of selected students. DAI, 37(4), 1992A.

666. Marx, M. R. (1984). The influence of counseling experience on the relationship between self-actualization and the ability to effectively communicate genuineness, empathy and positive regard. DAI, 45(5), 1300A.

667. Mase, B. F. (1971). Changes in self-actualization as a result of two types of residential group experience. DAI, 32(6), 3643B.

668. Maynard, C. K. (1984). Two information processing variables and self-actualization as predictors of clinical hypothesis formation. DAI, 45(9), 2765A.

669. Melchers, E. E. (1971). The value of the Personal Orientation Inventory in predicting counselor effectiveness and the value of a counseling practicum in promoting self-actualization. DAI, 32(7), 3696A.

670. Miller, C. H. (1977). An evaluation of the effect of the personal goals-setting element in the human potential seminar on growth toward self-actualization. DAI, 38(10), 5982A.

671. Miller, S. E. (1980). The effects of two group approaches, psychodrama and encounter, on levels of self-actualization: A comparative study. DAI, 41(6), 2456A.

672. Mirrow, G. S. (1977). A study of the effect of group counseling on the self-concept and level of self-actualization of high school students. DAI, 38(1), 5928A.

673. Montgomery, E. F. (1975). A study of the effects of career and personal group counseling on retention rates and self-actualization. DAI, 36(4), 2029A.

674. Musco, R. A. (1979). The effects of counselor-induced conditions of present-centeredness on self-actualization in college students. DAI, 39(12), 7164A.

675. Newcomb, J. K. (1983). Effects of counselor training on helping skills and self-actualization. DAI, 44(9), 2902B.

676. Nieuwoudt, W. C. (1980). A research into the relationship between mental health and self-actualization. DAI, 42(1), 146A.

677. O'Brien, E. B. (1976). Relationship of teachers' philosophy of human nature and self-actualization with perception of counselor role. DAI, 37(2), 814A.

678. Oliver, C. M. (1970). A study of the effects of behavior group counseling on self-actualization. DAI, 31(8), 3881A.

679. Ollerman, T. E. (1975). The effect of group counseling upon self-actualization. DAI, 36(6), 3415A.

680. Papantones, M. (1977). A Transactional Analysis group program designed to increase the self-actualization of adolescent males in a residential camp setting as measured by the Personal Orientation Inventory. DAI, 38(11), 6542A.

681. Papillon, S. (1977). Differential changes in self-actualization in external locus-of-control subjects after spaces-structures-group therapy. Unpublished doctoral dissertation, University of Ottawa, Canada.

682. Partin Jr., B. F. (1974). The relationship of Rorschach "M," origence, and intellectence to self-actualization, Rogers' facilitative conditions, and counselor effectiveness. DAI, 36(1), 135A.

683. Patterson, G. E. (1974). Time duration in marathon groups: Effects upon self-concept and self-actualization. DAI, 35(9), 5826A.

684. Pearson, P. T. (1973). The comparative effects of a cognitive and an affective counselor training program on the client-counselor relationship and counselor self-actualization. DAI, 34(7), 3886A.

685. Percy, L. E. (1978). An analysis of the relationship between self-actualization of counselor-trainees and counseling effectiveness as perceived by clients and supervisors. DAI, 40(2), 680A.

686. Perkins, R. J. (1979). Effects of peer counselor assertiveness training groups on levels of assertiveness and self-actualization. DAI, 40(5), 2338B.

687. Peterson, S. E. (1972). Growth in maturity, overall adjustment, and self-actualization of selected adolescents participating in three different group-counseling treatments. DAI, 33(11), 6183A.

688. Pertzborn, A. M (1979). The effect of gestalt therapy on self-actualization, anxiety and muscle tension in female college students. DAI, 41(3), 1123B.

689. Phillips, S. D. (1974). Self/ideal value congruence and its relationship to self-actualization and counseling effectiveness among selected counselor trainees. DAI, 35(4), 1987A.

690. Post Jr., H. H. (1969). Self-actualization and the interpersonal relationship environment. DAI, 31(1), 383B.

691. Puckett, J. R. (1977). The intimacy/individuation conflict: A study of the relationship between level of self-actualization and couple interaction. DAI, 38(6), 2880B.

692. Roberts, C. V. (1976). An investigation of the effect of a college group laboratory experience on measured levels of self actualization and interpersonal compatibility. DAI, 36(9), 5836A

693. Roberts, J. A. (1978). The effectiveness of the personal inventory blank approach in facilitating the self-actualization of counselor-trainees. DAI, 39(12), 7167A.

Self-Actualization

694. Robinson, S. G. C. (1983). The relationship between self-actualization repression-sensitization, and number and negative valuation of stressful life events. DAI, 45(5), 1431B.

695. Rodriguez, A. M. (1976). The relationship between a measure of self-actualization and the facilitative conditions offered in counseling. DAI, 37(8), 4872A.

696. Roe, R. F. (1980). The effects of a partnership counseling experience on the level of self-actualization of high school students. DAI, 41(9), 3889.

697. Rollins, J. A. (1968). Self-actualization and anxiety: Predictors of counseling effectiveness? DAI, 29(11), 3841A.

698. Rosenthal, S. W. (1976). Effects of psychodrama on self-actualization and perceived locus-of-control. DAI, 38(1), 378B.

699. Rowe, W. (1971). The effect of short-term group counseling and cognitive learning on a measure of self-actualization of counselors in training. DAI, 32(9), 4965A.

700. Rykiel, R. S. (1979). Alienation and self-actualization in mental health organizations. Unpublished doctoral dissertation, Fairleigh Dickinson University, New Jersey.

701. Saffell, S. M. A. (1979). An analysis of status variables and significant relationships between androgyny and self-actualization of counselors. DAI, 41(2), 540A.

702. Shanklin, P. A. (1983). The effects of a theme-centered group counseling experience on the self-concept and self-actualization of confined adolescent females. DAI, 44(11), 3290A.

Self-Actualization

703. Shoemaker, W. F. (1972). Changes in measured self-actualization as influenced by a group counseling procedure. DAI, 32(8), 4361A.

704. Smith, M. F. (1976). An investigation of the effects of a marathon group in a college dormitory setting on a measure of self-actualization. DAI, 37(7), 4146A.

705. Smith Jr., O. P. (1970). Changes in self-actualization and self-concept as a result of the uses of visual feedback in marathon sensitivity training. DAI, 31(7), 3280A.

706. Sobel, W. K. (1977). Sex-role stereotypes in relation to self-actualization and maternal employment among prospective clinicians. DAI, 38(6), 2950B.

707. Sparacio, R. T. (1980). The influence of counselor structure training on counselor-client relationship. DAI, 41(9), 3891A.

708. Stevens, J. L. (1983). Power animals, animal imagery, and self actualization. DAI, 45(2), 658B.

709. Strelich, T. J. (1976). Strengths enhancement training: Self-concept and self-actualization. DAI, 37(10), 5336B.

710. Tansey, F. M. (1979). Videotape focused feedback techniques in marathon group therapy: Effects on self-actualization and psychopathology. DAI, 39(11), 5592B.

711. Tchack, E. (1972). Self-actualization and clarity of perception of self and others during sensitivity training. DAI, 33(5), 2183A.

712. Travis III, W. P. (1976). Empathic understanding and self-actualization: A comparative study of rehabilitation counselors with different levels and patterns of education. DAI, 37(12), 7551A.

156

713.   Tucker, M. A. (1974). The effects of the human potential seminar upon counselor education students' level of self-actualization and ability to discriminate facilitative conditions. DAI, 34(12), 7541A.

714.   Uhren, K. K. (1981). The effects of three types of group counseling on the self-actualization, self-concept, and level of dogmatism of adolescents. DAI, 42(5), 2042A.

715.   Vance, E. M. B. (1967). Relationship of self-actualization to mental health. DAI, 28(1), 135A.

716.   Varner, F. B. (1969). Impact of basic group encounter on self-actualization of junior college students. DAI, 31(5), 2120A.

717.   Venino, W. K. (1973). A comparison of two encounter group approaches in promoting personal growth and self-actualization. DAI, 34(11), 6989A.

718.   Walder, J. M. (1975). The effects on a measure of self-actualization of adding a meditation exercise to a sensitivity group-group facilitator training program. DAI, 36(10), 6533.

719.   Walker, J. S. (1975). Effect of intensive group experiences on changes in measurers of self-actualization in Afro-American state university college students. DAI, 36(8), 4141B.

720.   Wanzek, R. P. (1971). A comparison of concepts of the healthy personality in contemporary social and phenomenological psychotherapy and representative contemporary theology. DAI, 33(7), 3412A.

721.   Warner, P. D. (1979). The usefulness of counselor training via a didactic-experiential interpersonal skills model for improving interpersonal relationships, counseling skills, and self-actualization of trainees. DAI, 40(3), 1371A.

722. Warner, S. G. (1979). The effects of human potential laboratory groups on self-actualization, self-esteem and anxiety. DAI, 40(7), 3794A.

723. Weinrach, S. G. (1972). The relationship between the level of counselor self-actualization and student perception of the guidance program. DAI, 33(9), 4860A.

724. Weinstein, C. G. (1975). Differential change in self-actualization and self-concept, and its effect on marital interaction, as an outcome of a selected growth group-experience. DAI, 36(6), 4067A.

725. Wemhoff, R. T. (1978). The effects of two different counseling orientations and procedures on self-actualization of group counseling participants. DAI, 39(6), 3386A.

726. Wilgus, E. D. (1981). Self-actualization and client-counselor relationships in a nursing student group experience. DAI, 42(2), 559A.

727. Williams, M. G. (1972). Selected scores of self-acceptance and self-actualization as predictors of counselor effectiveness. DAI, 33(4), 1776B.

728. Yiannikakis, E. E. (1976). Self-actualization, absorption, attitude toward hypnosis, sex, and hypnotic susceptibility in college students. DAI, 37(3), 1476A.

729. Young, S. O. (1974). Changes in self-concept and self-actualization of encounter group members as a correlate of the co-facilitator relationship. DAI, 35(12), 6122B.

730. Zelenski Jr., J. F. (1972). Factors influencing changes in affective sensitivity and self-actualization as the result of a T-group experience. DAI, 33(9), 4863A.

Self-Actualization

731. Zurflueh, M. (1974). An investigation of the relationship between self-disclosure, self-actualization, and counselor effectiveness. DAI, 34(10), 6472A.

Religion and self-actualization are related topics because characteristics of self-actualization such as peak experiences, values and a philosophy of life have religious meanings as well.. This section is devoted to those sources that deal directly with the relationship of self-actualization and religion. For further information on some other aspects of the relationship between self-actualization and religion see the sections on meditation, peak experiences and values.

732. Allport, G. W. (1963). Behavioral science, religion, and mental health. Journal of Religion and Health, 2, 187-197.

Suggests that an understanding of mental health requires metaphors of both hard science and of religion. The article discusses the place of religion in mental health, its merits and limitations, intrinsic and extrinsic religion and the problems of cooperation between religion and mental health science.

733. Bailey, L. W. (1975, Fall). Focus of fulfillment. Journal of Psychology and Theology, 3(4), 294-297.

Seeks to reconcile the dilemma of living a fulfilling, self-actualizing life while Christian theology teaches the denial of the self. The author finds a reconciliation in the teachings of Maslow in which the focus of self-actualization is outside the self in commitments and concern with others and the world-at-large.

734. Ellens, J. H. (1982, Fall). God's grace and human health: The biblical theological base. Journal of Psychology and Christianity, 1(3), 53-61.

Holds that the biblical implication of the teachings of the Bible is self-actualization. "Failure in that growth process is a failure of destiny and, therefore, sickness and sin."

735. Fuller, R. C. (1982, Fall). Carl Rogers, religion, and the role of psychology in American culture. Journal of Humanistic Psychology, 22(4), 21-32.

Responds to criticism of humanistic psychology as promoting the rise of narcissism through an examination of the writing of Carl Rogers. The author argues that Rogers' writings "have given psychological embodiment to the religious and ethical assumptions that have shaped the successive articulation of a peculiarly American spirituality."

736. Hamon, S. A. (1977, Fall). Beyond self-actualization: Comments on the life and death of Stephen The Martyr. Journal of Psychology and Theology, 5(4), 292-299.

Attempts to introduce the concept of Christian martyrdom as a proper study for psychology. The author advances the idea that Stephen, as discussed in the Book of Acts, surpasses Maslow's concept of self-actualization. The implications for Christian living are discussed.

737. Hjelle, L. A. (1975, March). Relationship of a measure of self-actualization to religious participation. Journal of Psychology, 89(2), 179-182.

Studied undergraduate male students enrolled in a co-educational Catholic institution for the relationship between self-actualization and participation in religious activities.

The study revealed a negative correlation between level of self-actualization, as measured by the POI, and active religious participation. The authors suggested that students with high levels of self-actualization construe participation in religious activities as "detrimental to their psychological development."

738. Hood Jr., R. W. (1977, Spring). Differential triggering of mystical experience as a function of self actualization. Review of Religious Research, 18(3), 264-270.

Investigated the different types of experiences that trigger or stimulate a mystical experience. The author studied 2 groups including both high and low self-actualizers. The results show that high self-actualizers tend to have mystical experiences triggered by drug or sexual experiences while low self-actualizers tend to have such experiences triggered by religious or nature settings.

739. Jansen, D. G. & Garvey, F. J. (1974, June). Self-actualization of clergymen rated high and low in clinical competencies. Counselor Education and Supervision, 13(4), 298-302.

Studied self-actualization in clergymen enrolled in a program of clinical pastoral education and sought to determine if differences were evident in those rated high or low in counseling competence. The results indicate clear differences between clergy rated high in competence and self-actualization and those rated low in competence and low in self-actualization. The authors suggest that the results of this study show that clergy who seek counselor training in secular graduate program need to have special programs different from standard programs since they have different vocational and personal needs.

740. Klingberg, H. E. (1973, October). An evaluation of sensitivity training effects on self-actualization, purpose in life, and religious attitudes of theological students. Journal of Psychology and Theology, 1(4), 31-39.

Outlines 7 problems of sensitivity training in the literature and examines the use of intensive groups at theological institutions. Also reports a research study in which 4 groups (2 professionally led, 1 self-directed and 1 control) are compared on changes in self-actualization, purpose in life and religious attitude. The results showed no significant changes.

741. Larsen, J. A. (1979, Spring). Self-actualization as related to frequency, range, and pattern of religious experience. Journal of Psychology and Theology, 7(1), 39-47.

Compared over 400 undergraduate students scores on 3 instruments measuring respectively self-actualization, personal data and religious experience. The results indicate that both high and low self-actualizers have religious experiences and that the presence or absence of such experiences cannot be viewed as indicators of pathology or of mental health. There were some differences reported in range and frequency.

742. Lee, R. & Piercy, F. P. (1974, September). Church attendance and self-actualization. Journal of College Student Personnel, 15(5), 400-403.

Studied the relationship to church attendance to self-actualization. The outcome was that infrequent church-goers tended to have higher self-actualization scores on the POI.

743. Lindskoog, D. & Kirk, R. E. (1975, March). Some life-history and attitudinal correlates of self-actualization among evangelical seminary students. Journal for the Scientific Study of Religion, 14(1), 51-55.

Sought to "determine religious and religiously neutral biographical correlates of self-actualization in evangelical seminary students." The study included such background factors as religious attitudes, beliefs, practices, political-social attitudes, family structure, demographics and level of moral development as well as self-actualization scores. Based on POI scores 3 groups were separated into high, moderate and low self-actualizers. "Differences among the actualization groups were found for denominational loyalty, ecumenical attitude, personal plans for church vocation, reported socio-economic level, status of mother's occupation, liberalness of political attitude on concrete issues, and birth order." Generally, high self-actualizers differed from other groups in degree of personal options, view of self as upwardly mobile, favoring social change and sense of freedom to depart from traditional methods in expressing their evangelical theology.

744. Maslow, A. H. (1969). Various meanings of transcendence. Journal of Transpersonal Psychology, 1, 56-66. (also in Pastoral Psychology, 19, 45-49.

Provides a descriptive listing of definitions of transcendence. Maslow provides a condensed statement of transcendence as "the very highest and most inclusive or holistic levels of human consciousness, behaving and relating as ends rather than as means, to oneself, to significant others, to human beings in general, to other species, to nature and to the cosmos."

745. Murphy, T. J. (1980, Summer). The relationship between self-actualization and adjustment among American Catholic priests. Educational and Psychological Measurement, 40(2), 457-461.

Studied the relationship between self-actualization and adjustment among American Catholic priests. There appeared to be a low positive correlation for adjustment of the priests with self-actualization.

746. Oakland, J. A. (1974, Summer). Self-actualization and sanctification. Journal of Psychology and Theology, 2(3), 202-209.

Attempts to connect the theological concept of sanctification, as viewed from a Reformed and Wesleyan perspective, with the psychological concept of self-actualization. The author uses Jesus Christ as the outstanding example of self-actualization and suggests that the study of santification in the history of Christianity provides clues to growth-oriented psychology.

747. Sobosan, J. G. (1977, October). Self-fulfillment, asceticism, and the function of authority. Journal of Religion and Health, 16(4), 333-340.

Argues that asceticism is a part of all human life and not just a concept for religious consideration. The author further concludes that the crisis in Christian thought is not so much a refusal to submit to authority as it is a lack of faith in persons in positions of authority to make decision that will enhance the self-fulfillment of individuals within the church.

748. Stones, C. R. (1982, May). A community of Jesus people in South Africa: Changes in self-actualization. Small Group Behavior, 13(2), 264-272.

Reported that a community of Jesus people (born-again Christians) had higher levels of self-actualization before their conversion experience and that their reported self-actualization decreased with participation in the Jesus community. It was suggested that perceived self-actualization may have gone down due to adherence to group norms. See also (749).

749. Stones, C. R. (1980, February). A Jesus community in South Africa: Self-actualization or need for security? Psychological Reports, 46(1), 287-290.

Compared self-actualizaton of a control group of mainstream-church denominational members with a group of Jesus people who had undergone "rapid and emotional conversions." It was found that the Jesus people were significantly more self-actualizing than the mainstream-church control group and that "perceived self-actualization decreased as a function of their religious experience." The author suggests that some perceived decline in self-actualization may be due to "rising expectations." See also (748).

Dissertations and Theses

750. Abbott, G. C. (1982). Personal and occupational self-actualization in the church. Unpublished doctoral disseration. North American Baptist Seminary, Souix Falls, South Dakota.

751. Barram, R. D. (1973). Mid-life transitional issues in the individuation of Protestant clergymen: An exploratory study. DAI, 45(12), 3928B.

752. Burke, J. F. (1973). The relationship between religious orientation and self-actualization among selected Catholic religious groups. DAI, 34(4), 1721B.

Self-Actualization

753. Day, L. G. (1980). The relationship of self-disclosure and self-actualization to cognitive and affective god concepts. DAI, 41(3), 1088B.

754. Dickson, E. J. (1978). Core religious experience and the process of self-actualization within the context of a religious congregation. Unpublished doctoral dissertation. University of Ottawa, Canada.

755. Elmo, F. E. (1974). The concept of self-actualization in the theology of Paul Tillich and the psychology of Abraham Maslow. DAI, 35(3), 1741A.

756. Galbreath, P. H. (1984). The Christology of the gospels and Abraham Maslow's characteristics of self-actualization. DAI, 45(4), 1134A.

757. Geary, T. F. (1975). Self-actualization in clinical pastoral education. DAI, 36(11), 5790B.

758. Hoover, E. A. (1977). Self-actualization, conservative ideology, congregational religious activity, and marital adjustment. DAI, 37(12), 7803A.

759. Klingberg Jr., H. E. (1971). An evaluation of sensitivity training effects on self-actualization, purpose in life, and religious attitudes of theological students. DAI, 32(12), 7312B.

760. Kowalski, J. (1984). The relationship between self-actualization and participation in congregation-sponsored growth programs for women within the Adrian Dominican congregation. DAI, 45(6), 1953B.

761. Krawinkel, R. M. (1977). Changes in self-actualization, self-concept and selected attitudes of Catholic seminarians as a function of field education. DAI, 38(9), 5374A.

Self-Actualization

762. Larsen, J. A. (1976). Self-actualization as related to frequency, range, and pattern of religious experience. DAI, 36(11), 5762B.

763. Panella, J. A. (1977). Self-actualization as a function of religious life-style. DAI, 38(9), 4476B.

764. Pothirajulu, D. (1978). An educational model of social self-actualization with strategies of adult laity formation and ministry in the church of South India. DAI, 40(2), 918A.

765. Reglin, R. (1976). A study of self-actualization factors in individuals with a conservative evangelical religious background. DAI, 37(2), 960B.

766. Reynolds, E. N. (1968). Interpersonal risk and self-actualization in four religious groups. DAI, 30(9), 4019A.

767. Sunderland, R. H. (1978). A study of relationships of dogmatism, self-actualization, values, and state-trait anxiety, in students entering a clinical pastoral education program. DAI, 39(7), 4162A.

Considering the theoretical importance of sex and its relationship to self-actualization, it is suprising that so little research and writing was found that directly related or studied the two together. This is an area of high interest in the world-at-large and one in which researchers and students could easily finds topics of study. It is an area that needs to be explored more thoroughly in self-actualization theory.

768. Paxton, A. L. & Turner, E. J. (1978, May). Self-actualization and sexual permissiveness, satisfaction, prudishness and drive among female undergraduates. Journal of Sex Research, 14(2), 65-80.

Examined the relationship of self-actualization to aspects of female sexuality. The aspects examined were "religiosity, age, major, grade, residence (on/off campus)... The results indicated that ... there was a significant relationship between self-actualization and sexual permissiveness, sexual satisfaction and prudishness."

769. Stock, M. (1967). Adolescent masturbation and the development of a mature personality. Catholic Psychological Record, 5(2), 158-166.

Presents the psychosexual stages of Freud and the psychosocial stages of Erikson and argues that masturbation interferes with the mature development of personality.

770. Waterman, C. K., Chiauzzi, E. & Gruenbaum, M. (1979, November). The relationship between sexual enjoyment and actualization of self and sexual partner. Journal of Sex Research, 15(4), 253-263.

Sought to demonstrate that previous research

relating female sexual enjoyment and self-actualization applied to males as well and that sexual enjoyment of males and females is related to the self-actualization of the partner. The results were not in the direction predicted. "Partners' self-actualization was correlated with several aspects of male sexual enjoyment. However, female sexual enjoyment was negatively correlated with partners' self-actualization."

The connection between sports and self-actualization has not been lost on writers. There is still a demand for studies relating the two areas of human concern. It appears certain that as the separation between mind and body are further narrowed that the relationship between using one's body in optimal ways will find increasing areas of study in the field of self-actualization research. The work reported here has barely begun the work that is necessary.

771. Barcus, C. G. & Bergeson, R. G. (1972). Survival training and mental health: A review. Therapeutic Recreation Journal, 6(1), 3-7.

Reviewed the literature of the value of survival training. A limited number of studies were found. These pointed to some positive mental health benefit of survival training. However, the authors criticize both the limited number and the methodological shortcomings of these and point to the need for research in this area.

772. Butterfield, G. Woods, R. (1980, Summer). Self actualization and improvement in tennis skills at summer camps for adolescents. Adolescence, 15(58), 429-434.

Related tennis skill with self-actualization. The results were mixed in two separate studies at a summer tennis camp. The authors attribute some differences to the time during the summer when the camp occurred.

773. Gundersheim, J. (1982, December). A comparison of male and female athletes and nonathletes on measures of self-actualization. Journal of Sport Behavior, 5(4), 186-201.

Compared male and female athletes from a number of different sports to nonathletes on levels of self-actualization. The results indicate that there is no difference among male athletes in different sports, no difference among female athletes in different sports, no difference in male and female athletes and male and female nonathletes. However, female athletes were significantly more self-actualizing than male athletes.

774. Gunn, S. L. (1977, August). Play and the fully functioning person. Rehabilitation Literature, 38(8), 257-259.

Examines the concept of the leisure specialist and points out the many advantages of this profession in dealing with persons. While many other professions have to deal with the negative influences in society, the leisure specialist can observe play directly, immediately and work to eliminate blocks to joyful play.

775. Ibrahim, H. & Morrison, N. (1976, March). Self-actualization and self-concept among athletes. Research Quarterly, 47(1), 68-79.

Compared high school and college, male and female athletes to nonathletes on levels of self-actualization and self-concept. The results show, in general, that athletes appear to be average in self-actualization and below average in self-concept.

776. Magill, R. A. (1975, October). Self-actualization and the college athlete. In Canadian Psycho-motor Learning and Sport Psychology Symposium (7), Mouvement 7 (pp. 395-398). Quebec, Canada: Association des professionnels de l'activit e physique du Quebec.

Compared varsity and "B" team college baseball players with norms for college students in the POI manual. There were no distinguishable differences between varsity and "B" team athletes. The college athletes tended to be more self-actualizing than the average college student.

777. Thirer, J. & Grabiner, M. D. (1980). Self actualization through Zen and the martial arts. Review of Sport and Leisure, 5, 79-92.

Compares the concept of self-actualization with the practice of the martial arts. The authors examine "the practical application of the philosophy of Zen to competition and physical activity." The authors conclude that the two concepts are highly related and suggest that applying the concepts to sports and physical activity is not difficult.

Dissertations and Theses

778. Bohlmann, N. R. (1986). Use of RET bibliotherapy to increase self-acceptance and self-actualization levels of runners. DAI, 46(8), 2191A.

779. Davis, R. W. (1972). The fear experience in rock climbing and its influence upon future self-actualization. DAI, 32(12), 6794A.

780. Gray, S. W. (1981). The relationship between self-actualization and leisure satisfaction. DAI, 42(6), 2560A.

781. Greentree III, I. S. (1977). Wilderness challenge training: The impact of programmmed environmental adversity upon adult self-actualization and interpersonal behavior. DAI, 39(1), 380B.

782. Gundershiem, J. (1978). A comparison of athletes and non-athletes on measures of self-actualization and sensation seeking. Unpublished doctoral disseration. Springfield College, Springfield, Massachusetts.

783. Hargadine, M. P. (1973). Relationships between measures of self-actualization and evaluations of scope of movement. DAI, 34(7), 3955A.

784. Jones, A. (1979). The effects of running on self-actualization on, motivation, and mood. DAI, 40(12), 6153A.

785. Kaplan, L. (1976). Self-actualization: Body image and body awareness. Unpublished docotral dissertation, California School of Professional Psychology, Berkeley.

786. Krause, M. A. (1980). The relationship between self-actualization and levels of involvement in running. DAI, 41(12), 4730B

787. Laffrey, S. C. (1982). Health behavior choice as related to self-actualization, body weight, and health conception. DAI, 43(11), 3536B.

788. Leiweke, J. T. (1976). The influence of the twenty-four day outward bound experience on self-actualization. DAI, 37(6), 3523A.

789. Moore III, J. E. (1975). The relationship between self-actualization and leisure activities. DAI, 35(7), 4675A.

790. Nelson, B. A. (1967). The relationship between selected aspects of self-actualization body and self-cathexis and two movement factors. DAI, 28(121), 4898A.

791. Ravizza, K. (1973). A study of the peak experience in sports. Unpublished doctoral dissertation. University of Southern California, Los Angeles, California.

792. Throneberry, C. A. (1979). A comparison of sex-role concepts and self-actualization of college female athletes and nonathletes. DAI, 40(12), 6193A.

Self-Actualization

793. Vogel, R. M. (1979). The effects of project use training (adventure training) on the participants' self-actualization and self-perception of personal change. DAI, 41(1), 173A.

This large section includes the philosophy, theory and a number of associations between self-actualization and other theoretical concepts. It includes the most important writings done on self-actualization by the major theorists in the field as well as important papers by less well-known writers who contribute considerably to the fund of knowledge concerning self-actualization. The philosophy and theory of self-actualization provides the underpinning for all other sections in this volume and is the touchstone for the research and speculation regarding psychological health from this orientation. To some extent, this section constitutes a mixed collection of research articles relating a theoretical position (eg, field independence or locus of control) to self-actualization, the very early writings of major theorists outlining the concept, modern papers updating early theory, and theoretical proposals outlining a theoretical position on the basic nature of human beings.

794. Alford, W. W. (1969, March). Essay on man: The search for total fulfillment. Peabody Journal of Education, 46(5), 282-287.

Presents an essay speculating on the potential of human beings for fulfillment. The essay is philosophical and religious in tone.

795. Ansbacher, H. L. (1978, Summer). Rogers' "formative tendency," Smuts, and Adler: A humanistic consensus. Journal of Humanistic Psychology, 18(3), 87-92.

Compares the "formative tendency" theory of Carl Rogers to the "holistic tendency" of Jan Smuts and the "striving toward completion" of Alfred Adler and concludes that all 3 have arrived at a "constructive tendency to counter the principle of entropy."

796. Barling, J. & Fincham, F. (1979, June). Maslow's need hierarchy and dimensions of perceived locus of control. Journal of Genetic Psychology, 134(2), 313-314.

Studied the relationship of locus of control to Maslow's hierarchy of needs. The findings indicated that externality was positively related to safety needs and internality was related to self-actualization. While caution was expressed, the authors linked internality to psychological health.

797. Bartley, S. H. (1982, August). Self-fulfillment. Perceptual and Motor Skills, 55(1), 326.

Argues that the concept of self-fulfillment cannot be conceived of in atomistic terms. To do so creates selfishness. The author presents an argument for the concept of "organicism" in which self-fulfillment is conceived of in wholistic terms and one which is more likely to result in an ideal society.

798. Bass, B. A. & Stek, R. J. (1972, October). Perceived locus of control and self-actualization: Failure to replicate. Perceptual and Motor Skills, 35(2), 646.

Failed to find a relationship between self-actualization scores and locus of control reported in previous research. The authors conclude that "at this stage, we can only state that the relationship between perceived locus of control and personal adjustment needs investigation." See Warehime & Foulds (909).

799. Bayne, R. (1977, June). What does self mean in the term self-actualization. Bulletin of the British Psychological Society, 30, 213-214.

Discusses the problem of the different meaning attributed to the term "self." The author separates the real self and the false self and further differentiates the real self in an effort of clarify the problem.

800. Biery, J. C. (1976). Can an engineer be actualized. Chemical Engineering Education, 10(2), 94-98.

Describes a senior seminar for chemical engineering students. The question "can an engineer be actualized" is discussed in the seminar and , the author reports, that no firm conclusion is reached in the seminar. The author concludes, for himself, a more hopeful outcome in which he sees the possibility of self-actualization for engineer in spite of the obstacles presented in engineering.

801. Blazer, J. (1963, Spring). An experimental evaluation of "transcendence of environment." Journal of Humanistic Psychology, 3, 49-53.

Tested whether higher self-actualizing persons were more likely to enjoy sensory deprivation. The results suggest "that the linear relationship found to exist in this study is indicative of a general trend for persons who are relatively more mature to adjust to relative sensory isolation and actually to find it more enjoyable than do persons of less general maturity."

802. Bonney, M. (1969, June). Self-becoming as self-growth. Theory Into Practice, 8(3), 143-148.

Based on the author's book (Bonney, M. (1969) The normal personality. Berkeley. California: McCutchan Publishing Corporation.) The author points out that self-actualization is not a static state but, rather, a continual process.

803. Bossom, J. & Maslow, A. H. (1957). Security of judges as a factor in impressions of warmth in others. Journal of Abnormal Social Psychology, 55, 147-148.

Studied the effect of personal security on making judgments of others. The results were that "the percentage of judges reporting Warm impressions more often than Cold impressions tended to be greater in the secure group than in the insecure group."

804. Braun, J. R. (1969, April). Search for correlates of self-actualization. Perceptual and Motor Skills, 28, 557-558.

Studied the correlations between accurate perception, logical reasoning and preference for ambigious and unstructured stimuli. The hypothesized positive correlation was not supported.

805. Brockett, C. (1975-1976). Toward a clarification of the need hierarchy theory: Some extensions of Maslow's conceptualization. Interpersonal Development, 6(2), 77-90.

Examines Maslow's hierarchy of needs with an emphasis on safety, belongingness/love and esteem. The author suggests that these needs, in particular, can be further divided into more precise qualitative hierarchies that lend themselves to more adequate research.

806. Butler, J. M. & Rice, L. N. (1963). Adience, self-actualization and drive theory. In J. M. Wepman and R. W. Heine (Eds.), Concepts of personality (pp.79-110). Chicago, Illinois: Aldine.

Provides a review of literature and theory regarding drive reduction theories which the authors do not reject but insist must be reformulated. Self-actualization as a concept is reviewed and its place as an outcome of psychotherapy is considered.

807. Butler, R. R. (1977, June). Self-actualizing: Myth or reality? Group and Organization Studies, 2(2), 228-233.

Reports a study in which the outcome of a semester-long, encounter-group, personal-growth-group in terms of movement in the direction of self-actualization. Both the control group and the experimental group showed gains in self-actualization. Reasons for this and suggestion for research strategies are offered.

808. Cangemi, J. P. (1976, May). Characteristics of self-actualizing individuals. Psychology, 13(2), 48-49.

Provides a list of characteristics of self-actualizing people. The list includes: superior judgment and wisdom, control of destiny, sure of self, intimate relations with others, unencumbered by expectations and obligations, more integrated and harmonious personality, reliable, trustworthy, dependable, committed to important jobs, highly independent and they have peak experience. The author provides no references or indication of the source of these characteristics.

809. Cangemi, J. & Englander, M. (1974). From self-awareness to self-actualization. College Student Journal, 8, 88-92.

Argues that self-awareness is "required for psychological growth." The article is written to support the idea that "self-actualization results from a process, and the foundation of the process is self-awareness."

810. Cangemi, J. P. & Martray, C. R. (1975, August). Awareness: A psychological requisite for the actualizing personality. Psychology, 12(3), 44-49.

Seeks to develop a model leading to self-actualization. The underpinning of the model is self-awareness.

811. Combs, A. W. (1961). What can man become? California Journal for Instructional Improvement, 4, 15-23.

Self-Actualization

Outlines the author's description of the self-actualizing person and provides implications for each of the attitudinal descriptions.

812. Cunningham, C. H., Wakefield Jr., J. A. & Ward, G. R. (1975, December). An empirical comparison of Maslow's and Murray's needs systems. Journal of Personality Assessment, 39(6), 594-596.

Studied the relationships of the theories of Maslow and Murray. Three relationships were found. "The first relationship supported Maslow's need hierarchy in general and its measurement by the WMI [Work Motivation Inventory]. The second suggested a fluctuating relationship between giving and receiving help and the levels of Maslow's hierarchy. The third relationship suggested that need for Achievement is associated with the intermediate levels of Maslow's hierarchy."

813. Daniels, M. (1982, January-April). The development of the concept of self-actualization in the writings of Abraham Maslow. Current Psychological Reviews, 2(1), 61-75.

Traces the development of Maslow's thinking about self-actualization through 4 decades of his writing. The author argues that Maslow never arrived at an overall, coherent theory and that the problem may have been in the approach Maslow took toward the investigation.

814. DiMarco, N. J. & Wilhelm, P. (1973, October). Relationship between self-actualization and manipulation. Psychological Reports, 33(2), 633-634.

Used the POI to measure self-actualization and the Mach IV to measure Machiavellianism. The results indicated some similarities between self-actualization and Machiavellianism and these were discussed.

181

815. Doyle, J. A. (1975, April). Field-independence and self-actualization. Psychological Reports, 36(2), 363-366.

Sought to correlate self-actualization scores with Witkin's rod and frame test of field independence/dependence. The results indicated 9 of 12 subscales of the POI were significantly and positively correlated with field independence.

816. Duck, L. E. (1977, Winter). Bronson Alcott, Abraham Maslow, and third force psychology. Education, 98(2), 210-220.

Reviews the work of the 19th Century educator Bronson Alcott whose ideas and practices appear to be antecedents to modern third force psychology and education according to the author.

817. Forest, J. J. & Sicz, G. (1981, Winter). Pseudo-self-actualization. Journal of Humanistic Psychology, 21(1), 77-83.

Examines the concept of pseudo-self-actualization which was originally proposed by ShostrOm in the 1966 Manual for the Personal Orientation Inventory (POI). Pseudo-self-actualization, as defined by ShostrOm, is a profile of exceedingly high scores on the POI. The authors describe the difficulties of the concept, point to a lack of a clear definition, difficulties of research and speculate that if such a concept were demonstrated it would throw into question much of the research which uses the Inner-Directed scale as a linear measure of self-actualization.

818. Frick, W. B. (1982, Fall). Conceptual foundations of self-actualization: A contribution to motivation theory. Journal of Humanistic Psychology, 22(4), 33-52.

Explores the idea that self-actualization is not an automatic outcome once the lower needs (physiological, safety, love, esteem) have been met. Points out that Maslow conceived of self-actualization as the weakest in the needs hierarchy. The author believes some additional explanation is needed to explain this phenomenon and seeks to provide a theory of "auxillary source of strength and support" for self-actualization to emerge. Essentially, the author proposes that it is necessary to develop a cognitive, conceptual scheme that "transmutes the primordial strivings toward growth into enlightened, focused, self-actualizing activity." The author suggests 5 components he feels are essential to this growth-enhancing conceptual understanding: ideal self, autonomy, life as process, interpersonal wholeness and community and the transpersonal realm.

819. Gilmore, J. V. (1971, October). The productive personality. Journal of Education, 154(1), 5-39.

Presents theory, concepts, and research describing the productive personality, which is the author's term for describing persons who have positive psychological development in 3 areas: academic achievement, creativity and/or leadership.

820. Goble, F. (1974, Summer). A note on self-actualization. Journal of Humanistic Psychology, 14(3), 75-77.

Argues that criticisms of the concept of self-actualization which attack it as a statement of fact are misguided since Maslow, as an example, did not state it as a fact but as a hypothesis. The author argues that this is in the best tradition of science.

821. Goldman, J. A. & Olczak, P. V. (1978, September). Self-actualization and impression formation. Journal of Personality, 46(3), 414-425.

Studied the relationship of self-actualization scores on the POI to 2 person perception experiments. "In general, self-actualized individuals were found to be more extreme in their responses to social stimuli than were non-self-actualizing individuals."

822. Goleman, D. (1975). Mental health in classical Buddhist psychology. Journal of Transpersonal Psychology, 7, 176-181.

Presents an overview of the characteristics viewed as psychologically healthy and unhealthy from Abhidhamma, the classical Buddhist psychology. The article discusses the 14 basic unhealthy factors as well as the 14 opposite healthy factors.

823. Graham, W. K. & Balloun, J. (1973, Winter). An empirical test of Maslow's need hierarchy theory. Journal of Humanistic Psychology, 13(1), 97-108.

Tested 2 hypotheses aimed at investigating the validity of Maslow's hierarchy of needs. Hypothesis 1 was that satisfaction of a need would be negatively correlated with desire for satisfaction of that need. Hypothesis 2 was that when two needs were compared the lower needs would show greater satisfaction. The results indicate partial support for both hypotheses.

824. Grinker, R. R. (1962). Mentally healthy young males (homoclites): A study. Archives of General Psychiatry, 6, 405-453.

Presents a thorough investigation into the mental health of a group of college males using a "multifaceted" research approach of observation, interviews, questionnaires and a behavior rating scale. Results are reported in description and statistical analyses to draw conclusions regarding mental health.

825. Grossack, M. M, Armstrong, T. & Lussiev, G. (1966, Spring). Correlates of self-actualization. Journal of Humanistic Psychology, 6(1), 87-88.

Correlated the POI with the Edwards Personal

Preference Schedule and the Cattell 16PF.

826. Groves, D. L., Kahalas, H. & Erickson D. L. (1975, Fall). A suggested modification to Maslow's need hierarchy. <u>Social Behavior and Personality</u>, <u>3</u>(1), 65-69.

Points out that problems of application have occurred in using Maslow's hierarchy especially at the upper levels. The authors sought to modify the hierarchy using concepts of power, competition, "other directed," and achievement. The authors suggest that the reason a person is at a particular level provides useful information.

827. Hageseth, J. A. & Schmidt, L. D. (1982, October). Self-actualization and conceptual structures. <u>Psychological Reports</u>, <u>51</u>(2), 672.

Sought to determine the relationship between conceptual abilities and self-actualization. The results show that self-actualization and conceptual abilities such as differentiation, integration and organization are positively related.

828. Hardeman, M. (1979, Winter). A dialogue with Abraham Maslow. <u>Journal of Humanistic Psychology</u>, <u>19</u>(1), 23-28.

Presents the transcript of Maslow's responses to student prepared questions when he visited the New School of Social Research in New York City.

829. Hayakawa, S. I. (1959). The fully functioning personality. In S. I. Hayakawa (Ed.), <u>Our language and our world</u> (pp. 202-217). New York: Harper and Row.

Outlines the theories of Carl Rogers and Abraham Maslow in describing the fully functioning personality or self-actualizing person. Hayakawa describes the characteristics contributed by Rogers and Maslow and comments on each.

830. Hjelle, L. A. (1976, June). Self-actualization and perceived locus of control: A comparison of relationships based on separate locus of control measures. <u>Journal of Genetic Psychology</u>, 128(2), 303-304.

Sought to determine the relationship of locus of control, using two different measures, to self-actualization. The relationship of self-actualization to internal locus of control was established . However, the Adult Nowicki-Strickland scale compared far more favorably than the Rotter I-E scale.

831. Hogan, H. W. & McWilliams, J. M. (1978, September). Factors related to self-actualization. <u>Journal of Psychology</u>, <u>100</u>, 117-122.

Study found females scoring higher than males on self-actualization, a negative correlation between self-actualization and perceived undesirable body image and, contrary to expectation, a negative correlation between self-actualization and androgyny. The authors discuss the implications of these results.

832. Huber, R. J. & Steier, R. (1976, April). Social interest and individuation: A comparison of Jung and Adler. <u>Character Potential</u>, <u>7</u>(4), 174-180.

Points out the differences (Jung emphasizes unconscious processes while Adler emphasizes conscious processes) and similarities (empathy and co-operation) between Jung and Adler in their understanding of mental health. The authors offer the concepts of Adler's social interest and Jung's individuation as a bridge between the 2 theories and suggest how these 2 theories can aid modern psychologists.

833. Kagel, R. O. & Crummett, W. B. (1978). Self-actualization and the analytical chemist. <u>Journal of Chemical Education</u>, <u>55</u>(5), 312-313.

Describes a procedure used to train and assess analytical chemists' technical competence and equates this gain in technical knowledge with one aspect of self-actualization.

834. Kinder, B. N. (1976, April). Evidence for a nonlinear relationship between self-disclosure and self-actualization. Psychological Reports, 38(2), 631-634.

Sought to establish a relationship between self-disclosure and self-actualization. The results indicate that "significant linear and nonlinear components were found when scores on the Personal Orientation Inventory Inner-directed scale were correlated with Jourard Self-disclosure Scale scores." These results were not apparent on the Time Competence subscale of the POI. Thus, there is support of the concept of a curvilinear relationship between self-disclosure and self-actualization (low self-actualizers both disclose too much or too little).

835. Landsman, T. (1969). The beautiful person. The Futurist, 3, 41-42.

Presents an overview of psychological health in 3 levels: the passionate self (positive self-regard), the productive person (fully functioning persons) and the compassionate person (loving). The author provides a description of each level as well as discussing significant events in the lives of persons that may have contributed to developing psychological health.

834. Leak, G. K. & McCarthy, K. (1984, November). Relationship between Type A behavior subscales and measures of positive mental health. Journal of Clinical Psychology, 40(6), 1406-1408.

Studied the relationship between self-actualization and self-esteem and Type A behavior. The results show that self-actualization and self-esteem are related to only one aspect of Type A behavior and suggestions are made for improving the Jenkins Activity Survey as a measure of Type A behavior.

837. Lombardo, J. P. & Fantasia, S. C. (1976, October). The relationship of self-disclosure to personality, adjustment, and self-actualization. Journal of Clinical Psychology, 32(4), 765-769.

Studied the relationship between self-disclosure and several measures of personality including self-actualization. The findings indicate a consistent relationship between high self-disclosure and positive personality variables such as self-disclosure.

838. Lomranz, J., Medini, G. & Aschuach, R. (1982, January). Realism as a cognitive indicator of self-actualization in temporality. Journal of Psychology, 110(1), 53-62.

Related discrepancies in present-future perceived self-actualization with Lewin's "realism." The results show that the higher one's cognitive realism the lower was the perceived sense of discrepancy in self-actualization.

839. Mahoney, J. & Hartnett, J. (1973, September). Self-actualization and self-ideal discrepancy. Journal of Psychology, 85(1), 37-42.

Used the Time Competence scale of the POI to measure self-actualization and the Interpersonal Check List to measure real and ideal self-concept. The outcome was that the higher the self-actualization score the less discrepancy there was between real and ideal self.

840. Marks, S. (1979, Summer). Culture, human energy, and self-actualization: A sociological offering to humanistic Psychology. Journal of Humanistic Psychology, 19(3), 27-42.

Argues that self-actualization does not have to be a characteristic that is culturally transcending but that cultures can seek to develop self-actualization in its members. The author presents descriptions of sacralizing cultures that promote and enhance altered states of consciousness that transcend the world and then contribute the gained knowledge to the culture.

841. Maslow, A. H. (1971, September-October). Personality problems and personality growth. College Student Journal, 5(2), 1-13.

Provides an overview of Maslow's thinking regarding personality development. The article gives 9 principles of Maslow's psychology as an outline for persons seeking to help themselves through personality problems.

842. Maslow, A. H. (1969, Spring). The farther reaches of human nature. Journal of Transpersonal Psychology, 1, 1-9.

Outlines the impact of the humanistic revolution on human concerns such as work, leisure, education, social institutions, science, philosophy and religion. Maslow makes the point that these changes are not of an organized nature but carried out by persons unknown to one another and have the character of a Zeitgeist, an age, a groundswell or a movement.

843. Maslow, A. H. (1967). Self-actualization and beyond. In J. F. T. Bugenthal (Ed.), Challenges of humanistic psychology (pp. 279-286). New York: McGraw Hill. Also reprinted in D. Hamachek (Ed.) (1968) Human dynamics in psychology and education. Boston: Allyn and Bacon.

Discusses some early history of Maslow's beginning research in self-actualization and provides a description of the behaviors leading up to self-actualization and speculates on self-actualization as a matter of daily living.

844. Maslow, A. H. (1965). Criteria for judging needs to be instinctoid. In M. R. Jones (Ed.), Human Motivation: A symposium (pp. 33-48). Lincoln, Nebraska: University of Nebraska Press.

Re-examines the theory of the instinctoid nature of basic needs and lists and discusses 18 definitions that identify a need as instinctoid.

845. Maslow, A. H. (1964). The superior person. Trans-action, 1, 10-13.

Advances what the author terms an "unpopular" idea in any democracy - that of the superior person. Maslow argues that there exist persons who are generally superior and it would be beneficial in a society to determine how to get these people into positions of leadership. "The implication of the existence of the generally superior person are fantastic and dangerous and perhaps more than a little frightening in a democracy."

846. Maslow, A. H. (1964). Synergy in the society and in the individual. Journal of Individual Psychology, 20, 153-164.

Describes the concept of synergy which the author credits to Ruth Benedict. "The writer of the present paper goes on to show how synergy is variously incorporated in our culture, in economic and managerial situations as well as interpersonal relationships and intrapersonally, and in each case high synergy corresponds to a fusion of what the individual wants personally with what is good for him and at the same time good for others."

847. Maslow, A. H. (1964/1965). Notes on innocent cognition. Explorations, 1, 2-8.

    "A distinction is made between the innocent, concrete cognition of suchness of (1) the child, who is not yet able to abstract, (2) of the brain-injured, who has lost the ability to abstract and is thereby reduced to the concrete, and (3) of the wise, healthy and mature man who is able to perceive concretely and also to unify the concrete with the abstract, the temporal with the eternal, the realm of deficiencies with the realm of Being (unitive consciousness)."

848. Maslow, A. H. (1964, Spring). Further notes on the psychology of being. Journal of Humanistic Psychology, 4, 45-58.

    Expands the writings on the concept of the psychology of Being. This article provides more detail on Synergy and especially on the resolution and transcendence of dichotomies.

849. Maslow, A. H. (1963). The need to know and the fear of knowing. Journal of General Psychology, 68, 111-125.

    Argues that human nature has within it a simultaneous, instinct-like need to know - that is to investigate, gain knowledge or skills or simply explore - as well as a need to be safe, protected. This need to know and the fear of knowing is affected by the physical and psychological environment to the extent that "social factors that increase fear will cut our impulse to know; all factors that permit courage, freedom and boldness will thereby also free our need to know."

850. Maslow, A. H. (1962, Fall). Notes on being-psychology. Journal of Humanistic Psychology, 2, 47-71.

    Provides a series of definitional statements outlining the nature, subject matter and concerns of Being psychology.

851. Maslow, A. H. (1961, Spring). Eupsychia - the good society. Journal of Humanistic Psychology, 1, 1-11.

Based on a radio interview and presented in transcribed form, this article discusses Maslow's views of a utopian society he labels Eupsychia.

852. Maslow, A. H. (1961, Fall). Health as transcendence of environment, Journal of Humanistic Psychology, 1, 1-7. Reprinted in (1968). Pastoral Psychology, 19, 45-49.

Argues that there is danger of the theory of adjustment to society as overwhelming the actualizing idea that psychological health can transcend the environment. Maslow holds that we cannot simply judge human worth in terms of each persons' worth to the society. Finally, he holds out for a unique position for psychology in understanding human functioning.

853. Maslow, A. H. (1957). Two kinds of cognition and their integration. General Semantics Bulletin, 20 & 21, 17-22. Reprinted in (1968). New Era in Home and School, 39, 202-205.

Argues that a merely rational approach or a merely intuitive approach to understanding the world is doomed to failure since it always leaves out something. "Only by resolving and transcending the dichotomy between primary and secondary processes, conscious and unconscious, rational and intuitive, scientific and aesthetic, work and play, abstracted and concrete, rubricizing and direct experiencing, can we perceive all of the world and of ourselves. Only thereby can we create whole-science, whole-language, whole-mathematics, whole-art, whole-education, and whole-people."

854. Maslow, A. H. (1956). Defense and growth.
      Merrill-Palmer Quarterly, 3, 36-47.
      Reprinted in T. Millon (Ed.), (1967).
      Theories of psychopathology. Philadelphia,
      Pennsylvania: Saunders.

      Attempts to describe in concrete detail how a
      child might move from spontaneous exploration
      to self-actualization.

855. Maslow, A. H. (1956). Self-actualizing
      people: A study of psychological health. In
      C. Moustakas (Ed.), The self (pp. 160-194).
      New York: Harpers and Row. Also in (1950).
      Personality symposia: Symposium #1 on values.
      New York: Grune and Stratton and (1963). G.
      B. Levitas (ed.), The world of psychology.
      New York: George Braziller and (1964). C. G.
      Kemp (Ed.), Perspective on the Group Process.
      New York: Houghton-Mifflin.

      Presents Maslow's characteristics of the
      self-actualizing person in its most concise
      form.

856. Maslow, A. H. (1955). Deficiency motivation
      and growth motivation. In M. R. Jones (Ed.),
      Nebraska symposium on motivation (pp. 1-30).
      Lincoln, Nebraska: University of Nebraska
      Press.

      Provides a background of Maslow's work to
      this point in his career and describes the
      self-actualizing characteristics, defines
      instinctoid, discusses deficiency and growth
      motivation and ends with the differences in
      Deficiency love and Being love. In this work
      see also comments on this article by David C.
      McClelland (pp. 31-37) and James Olds (pp.
      37-39).

857. Maslow, A. H. (1954). The instinctoid
      nature of basic needs. Journal of
      Personality, 22, 326-347.

      Re-examines instinct theory, argues against
      cultural relativism and makes a case of
      investigating the possibility of universal

human needs that transcend cultures. Maslow argues that in sum human beings have been underrated and undervalued by current scientific approaches and theories.

858. Maslow, A. H. (1951). Resistance to acculturation. Journal of Social Issues, 7, 26-29.

Suggests that self-actualization and adjustment to culture are two different concepts and that a self-actualizing person may not be well-adjusted. The author identifies the ways in which these differences may manifest themselves and provides a discussion of psychological health in an unhealthy society.

859. Maslow, A. H. (1951). Higher needs and personality. Dialectica, 5, 257-265.

Argues first that the "higher" needs are as "instinctoid" and characteristic of the human species as the needs for food, water, sex, etc. The author then presents 8 arguments supporting and defining the importance of "higher" needs in human beings.

860. Maslow, A. H. (1949). Our maligned animal nature. Journal of Psychology, 28, 273-278. Reprinted in (1953). S. Koenig et al (Eds.), Sociology: A book of readings. Englewood Cliffs, N.J.: Prentice-Hall.

Uses quotations from a book by M. E. Harding (1947, Psychic energy. Washington, D. C.: Pantheon Books.) to take issue with those who would view human and animal nature as evil, selfish, destructive, criminal and the like. Maslow uses the quotations to present his own more hopeful view of human nature and discusses the implications of accepting one point of view over the other.

861. Maslow, A. H. (1948). Some theoretical consequences of basic need-gratification. Journal of Personality, 16, 402-416.

Provides an overview of the theory of basic need gratification as well as a discussion of the outcome of need gratification and of the shortcomings of the theory.

862. Maslow, A. H. (1948). "Higher" and "lower" needs. Journal of Psychology, 25, 433-436.

Attempts to demonstrate "'real' psychological and operational differences" between "higher" and "lower" needs. The author further argues that this would serve to establish a values hierarchy within the organism itself and that science, especially psychology, in refusing to consider values weakens itself.

863. Maslow, A. H. (1946). Problem-centering vs. means-centering in science. Philosophy of Science, 13, 326-331.

Stresses that a "too exclusive concern with method, instrument, technique or procedure fosters" mistakes such as valuing technique over creativeness and significance, promoting technicians rather than discovers, fitting problems to techniques and neglect of problem of values as well as other problems not listed here.

864. Maslow, A. H. (1943). A theory of human motivation. Psychological Review, 50, 370-396. Reprinted many times over the years.

Presents Maslow's now famous hierarchy of needs and discusses the implications of the theory for psychology and the larger society.

865. Maslow, A. H. (1943). The dynamics of personality organization (Parts I & II). Psychological Review, 50, 514-539, 541-558.

Presents a thorough, detailed and "not a theoretical paper, in the ordinary sense, but rather a set of theoretical conclusions emerging directly from research data on the organization of the human personality" and argues for a holistic-analytical method rather than a reductionistic one.

866. Maslow, A. H. (1943). A preface to motivation theory. Psychosomatic Medicine, 5, 85-92.

    Gives 13 propositions Maslow believes must be incorporated into any comprehensive theory of personality and discusses each.

867. Maslow, A. H. (1942). The dynamics of psychological security-insecurity. Character and Personality, 10, 331-344.

    Classifies security-insecurity as a syndrome and provides 14 characteristics of security and 14 corresponding and opposite characteristics for insecurity. The author then provides a detailed description of the dynamics of the development of security-insecurity feelings.

868. Mathes, E. W. (1981, Fall). Maslow's hierarchy of needs as a guide for living. Journal of Humanistic Psychology, 21(4), 69-72.

    Tested the hypothesis that people unknowingly use Maslow's hierarchy of needs in their daily living. The author developed a questionnaire of forced choices between a higher need and a lower need. This questionnaire was given to subjects unfamiliar with Maslow's work. The hypothesis was not supported and explanations for the reasons are given in the article.

869. Mathes, E. W. & Edwards, L. L. An empirical test of Maslow's theory of motivation. Journal of Humanistic Psychology, 18(1), 75-77.

    Tested Maslow's needs for hierarchical accuracy. "The results of this study suggest that Maslow's hierarchical theory of motivation should be modified to include only two or three levels. Security was shown to be a prerequisite to self-actualization, while belongingness and esteem were shown not to be essential prerequisites."

870. Metzner, R. (1980). Ten classical metaphors of self-transformation. Journal of Transpersonal Psychology, 12(1), 47-62.

Provides the reader with 10 metaphors of personal transformation such as from dream-sleep to awakening.

871. Moore, J. A. & Sermat, V. (1974, June). Relationship between self-actualization and self-reported loneliness. Canadian Counsellor, 8(3), 194-196.

Tested the hypothesis that persons who identified themselves as less lonely would be higher in self-actualization than those who identified themselves as more lonely. The hypothesis was confirmed.

872. Niemeier, D. L. & Douglass, H. J. (1975, April). Transactions and self-actualization. Transactional Analysis Journal, 5(2), 152-157.

Concerned with relating the theory of Transactional Analysis to the concept of self-actualization. The study hypothesized that self-actualization would be related to the adult-adult transaction rather than the adult-child, child-adult type of transaction. The hypothesis was supported.

873. O'Byrne, M. M & Angers, W. P. (1972) Jung's concept of self-actualization and Teilhard De Chardin's philosophy. Journal of Religion and Health, 11(3), 241-251.

Compares and contrast the writings of Jung, the psychologist, and Teilhard De Chardin, the philosopher. The authors conclude that the two share many similarities especially their concern with the spiritual aspects of humanity and a believe that within human beings is a "drive" to move toward that spirituality (or humanity).

874. Olczak, P. V. & Goldman, J. A. (1978, May). Self-actualization and fear of incompetence. Psychology, 15(2), 37-41.

Hypothesized that persons with high self-actualization scores on the POI would show less fear of appearing incompetent in public. To test the hypothesis, the authors used the Good and Good Fear of Appearing Incompetent Scale along with the POI. The hypothesis was confirmed.

875. Olczak, P. V. & Goldman, J. A. (1975, March). Self-actualization as a moderator of the relationship between attitude similarity and attraction. Journal of Psychology, 89(2), 195-202.

Studied whether self-actualization was related to attraction and similarity or difference. The outcome was that subjects with higher self-actualization scores tended to rate strangers higher in attraction who had high levels of similarity and significantly lower in attraction those individuals with low levels of similarity than subjects with lower self-actualization scores.

876. Olczak, P. V. & Goldman, J. A. (1975, July). The relationship between self-actualization and psychosocial maturity. Journal of Clinical Psychology, 31(3), 415-419.

Compared scores on the POI with scores on a measure of Erikson's psychosocial maturity, the Inventory of Psychosocial Development (IPD). The results indicate a high significant relationship between the 2 test scores.

877. Otto, H. A. (1970, October). New light on the human potential. Childhood Education, 47(1), 23-28.

Reviews "indicators of the human potential" such as hypnosis, parapsychology, creativity and late-in-life talents.

Self-Actualization

878. Patterson, C. H. (1974). Beyond Competence: Self-actualization as an integrative concept. Counseling Psychologist, 4(4), 82-86.

Provides an overview of descriptions of self-actualization from several theorists and seeks to correct some misconceptions concerning self-actualization.

879. Petosa, R. (1984, May-June). Self-actualization and health related practices. Health Education, 15(3), 9-12.

Compared scores on the POI with life-style health practices as measured by the Health Practices Inventory (HPI). The results show that persons with healthier life-style practices tend to have higher self-actualization scores.

880. Piechowski, M. M. (1978, May). Self-actualization as a developmental structure: A profile of Antoine de Saint-Exupery. Genetic Psychology Monographs, 97(2),, 181-242.

Presents 113 fragments of de Saint-Exupery's writings as a basis for a profile of self-actualization using Maslow's characteristics as criteria. The author also points up the correspondence between self-actualization and Dabrowski's concept of positive disintegration.

881. Piechowski, M. M. & Tyska, C. A. (1982, February). Self-actualization profile of Eleanor Roosevelt- a presumed nontranscender. Genetic Psychology Monographs, 105(1), 95-153.

A thorough self-actualization profile of Eleanor Roosevelt using Maslow's characteristics as a basis for the profile.

882. Phillips, W. M., Watkins, J. T. & Noll, G. (1974, Summer). Self-actualization, self-transcendence, and personal philosophy. Journal of Humanistic Psychology, 14(3), 53-75.

Describes and contrasts the theories of Maslow and Frankl, operationally defines the 2 theories and presents a research study to test the hypothesis that the operational definitions describe the same individuals. Four separate test instruments were used: the POI as a measure of self-actualization, the Purpose-in-Life Test (PIL) to get at Frankl concept of the existential vacuum, the Personal Theoretical Orientation to Experience Questionnaire (PTOE) developed to force a choice by the subject between Maslow's and Frankl's theoretical orientation and the Conceptual Systems Test (CST) to measure conceptual openness. While many relationships were examined in this study, the overall thesis that, in spite of the theoretical differences of Maslow and Frankl, they are describing the same individuals was supported.

883. Price, D. Z. (1973, September). Relationship of decision styles and self-actualization. <u>Home Economics Research Journal</u>, <u>2</u>(1), 12-20.

Reported a study in which it was discovered that decision making style was related to level of self-actualization. The two styles tended to be traditional for "normal" and low self-actualizing people and "unorthodox" for high self-actualizing people. The author discusses the implications of this discovery.

884. Rizzo, R. & Vinacke, E. (1975, Summer). Self-actualization and the meaning of critical experience. <u>Journal of Humanistic Psychology</u>, <u>15</u>(3), 19-30.

Studied "most important" life events of students, mature adults and older people as they related to level of self-actualization. The outcome demonstrated that persons who report their most important personal experience as overall positive tended to show greater self-actualization than persons who reported their most important life experience as overall negative. The authors also discuss the usefulness of the POI as a measure of self-actualization for an older population.

885. Rogers, C. R. (1978, Winter). The formative tendency. Journal of Humanistic Psychology, 18(1), 23-26.

Outlines Rogers' thoughts on the "formative tendency" which he views as functioning in the universe at large as well as within individual human beings. The author argues that physical science has paid too much attention to the concept of entropy and not enough on the formative tendency. Rogers presents evidence from a number of different sources to back up his understanding of the formative tendency.

886. Rogers, C. R. (1973, Spring-Summer). To be fully alive. Penney's Forum, 3.

Outline Rogers' characteristics of the fully functioning person.

887. Rogers, C. R. (1972, Fall). The person of tomorrow. Colorado Journal of Educational Research, 12(1), 30-32.

Describes Rogers' views of the changing values, behaviors and beliefs of the coming generation as observed in a commencement address at Sonoma State College in June 1969.

888. Rogers, C. R. (1965). A humanistic conception of man. In R. E. Farson (Ed.), Science and human affairs (pp. 18-31). Palo Alto, California: Science and Behavior Books.

Describes Rogers' theories regarding the nature of human beings in a statement that reflects his views in the mid 1960's.

889. Rogers, C. R. (1963). The actualizing
tendency in relation to "motive" and to
consciousness. In M. R. Jones (Ed.),
Nebraska symposium on motivation (pp. 1-24).
Lincoln, Nebraska: University of Nebraska
Press.

Develops the idea of the actualizing tendency
and it relationship to motivation. Rogers
presents 3 main ideas in this article.
"First, there is a tendency toward
fulfillment which is the most basic aspect of
the life of any organism. It is the
substratum of anything we might term
motivation." Second, Rogers questions the
entire concept of motives. Third, he argues
that the bifurcated, dualistic understanding
of the world taught in, especially, Western
societies is not necessary, opposite of
nature and can be unlearned.

890. Rogers, C. R. (1963) The concept of the
fully functioning person. Psychotherapy:
Theory, Research and Practice, 1, 17-26.

Develops in detail Rogers' theoretical model
of the general characteristics of the healthy
personality which he identifies as the fully
functioning person.

891 Rogers, C. R. (1956). What it means to
become a person. In C. E. Moustakas (Ed.),
The Self (195-211). New York: Harper and
Row.

Uses client interviews to present the
author's theory and description of the fully
functioning, self-actualizing person.

892. Rogers, C. R. (1956). Becoming a person.
Pastoral Psychology, 7(61), 9-13. Also,
(1954). Oberlin College Nellie Heldt Lecture
Series. Oberlin, Ohio: Oberlin Printing Co.
and in S. Doniger (Ed.), (1957). Healing,
human and divine. New York: Association
Press.

Describes the climate necessary in order for

a person to develop most advantageously. This climate is characterized by genuineness and transparency, warm acceptance and sensitive ability to understand the other (congruence, positive regard and empathy).

893. Roweton, W. E. (1981, Fall). Who is self-actualized? Contemporary Education, 53(1), 22-25.

Reports a study in which students attributed qualities of self-actualization not so much to great historical figures as to neighbors, friends, relatives and other "ordinary" people. The author speculates about the meaning of this information.

894. Sandven, J. (1979). Conditions for self-realization: A theoretical discussion. Scandinavian Journal of Educational Research, 23(1), 15-30.

Discusses a proposed theory that for self-realization to occur there must be a correspondence between progress/achievement and potential or potentials. In order for this to occur, there must be a balance between protection and challenge.

895. Schuller, R. M. & Cangemi, J. P. (1978, Fall). A military approach to Maslow's hierarchy of needs. Journal of Instructional Psychology, 5(4), 13-21.

Attempts to simplify Maslow's theory of the hierarchy of needs to make it useful and practical to military personnel by applying it to a military weapons system.

896. Schwarta, M. M. & Gaines, L. S. (1974, October). Self-actualization and the human tendency for varied experience. Journal of Personality Assessment, 38(5), 423-427.

Examined whether self-actualization may be a form of human seeking for varied stimulation. Self-actualizers differ on the amount but not the variety of stimulation sought.

897. Schwitzgebel, R. (1961). The self in self-actualization. Psychologica, 4, 163-169.

Theoretical discussion of the definition of the self. The author provides a background of the study of the self in psychology and offers 4 descriptive propositions of the self for discussion and research.

898. Shoben Jr., E. J. (1967). Toward a concept of the normal personality. American Psychologist, 12(4), 183-189.

Offers a model of mental health "characterized by self-control, personal responsibility, social responsibility, democratic social interest, and ideals."

899. Shorkey, C. T. & Reyes, E. (1978, June). Relationship between self-actualization and rational thinking. Psychological Reports, 42(3, Pt. 1), 842.

Investigated the relationship between self-actualization, using the POI, and rational thinking, using the Rational Behavior Inventory (RBI). The hypothesized relationship between rational thinking and self-actualization was supported at the moderate to low level.

900. Smith, M. B. (1961). Mental health reconsidered: A special case of the problem of values in psychology. American Psychologist, 16, 299-306.

Argues that the problem of values in defining mental health may not be avoidable. The author goes on the argue that we should get over our embarrassment as psychologists about the intrusion of values into the criteria for mental health so long as it is made explicit. This may even be necessary.

901. Smith, M. B. (1959). Research strategies toward a conception of mental health. American Psychologist, 14, 673-681.

Self-Actualization

Provides an overview of the problems of research into mental health as well as offering several research strategies for approaching the investigation. The author concludes with a discussion of the value of systems theory in mental health research.

902. Smith, M. B. (1950). Optima of mental health. Psychiatry, 13, 503-510.

Suggests "a frame of reference for the analysis of mental health both within and between cultures, that may pose significant problems for research and help separate empirical questions from value judgments in this difficult area." The author proposes a triple criteria for mental health: adjustment, integration and cognitive adequacy.

903. Stark, M. J. & Washburn, M. C. (1977, January). Beyond the norm: A speculative model of self-realization. Journal of Religion and Health, 16(1), 58-68.

Provides a theory of self-realization and characteristics of self-realization that is a synthesis of a number of other theorists.

904. Szent-Gyoergyi, A. (1966). Drive in living matter to perfect itself. Individual Psychology, 22, 153-162.

Offers the theory, after 50 years of biological research, of a Nobel prize winning bichemist, that there exists "an innate drive in living matter to perfect itself," a "drive to improvement, to building up." Originally, printed under the title "Fifty Years of Poaching in Science," in The Graduate Faculties Newsletter, Columbia University, March 1966, pp. 1-5.

905. Szura, J. P. & Vermillion, M. E. (1975, October). Effects of defensiveness and self-actualization on a Herzberg replication. Journal of Vocational Behavior, 7(2), 181-186.

205

Tested the motivator (intrinsic)-hygiene (extrinsic) theory of job satisfaction with self-actualization. "Results indicate that self-actualization is related to the attribution of satisfaction to both motivators and hygienes and that external locus of control, sensitization, and low need for approval are related to the attribution of dissatisfaction to motivators and hygienes."

906. Stewart, R. A. (1974, September). States of human realization: Some physiological and psychological correlates. Psychologia: An International Journal of Psychology in the Orient, 17(3), 126-134.

Looks at several Eastern practices such as Zen, Yoga, biofeedback and especially Transcendental Meditation as they relate to self-realization.

907. Vinacke, W. E. (1984, May). Healthy personality: Toward a unified theory. Genetic Psychology Monograms, 109(2), 279-329.

Argues that healthy personality is as identifiable a pattern as any other in psychology that lends itself to a diagnostic category and that healthy personality is not simply "normality." "Four major pathways in development are outlined to highlight how health differs from other patterns."

908. Wall, J. B. (1970). Relationship of locus of control to self-actualization. Psychological Reports, 27, 282.

Compared scores on Rotter's Internal vs. External Control Scale with the POI. The author concludes that locus of control is a relatively independent concept from self-actualization.

909. Warehime, R. G. & Foulds, M. L. (1971). Perceived locus of control and personal adjustment. Journal of Consulting and Clinical Psychology, 37, 250-252.

Investigated the relationship of locus of control to self-actualization. The author found a significant relationship to internal locus of control for females but not for males. See (798).

910. Warehime, R. G., Routh, D. K. & Foulds, M. L. (1974, July). Knowledge about self-actualization and the presentation of self as self-actualized. Journal of Personality and Social Psychology, 30(1), 155-162.

Studied the effect of trying to fake on the POI. Subjects who were given information about self-actualization were able to raise their scores when asked to do so. However, when asked to respond honestly their scores did not show such influence.

911. Wexler, D. A. (1974, February). Self-actualization and cognitive processes. Journal of Consulting and Clinical Psychology, 42(1), 47-53.

"Investigated the hypotheses that (a) the creation of new experience in cognitive functioning involves increased differentiation and integration of meaning and (b) self-actualization involves the tendency to engage in a mode of cognitive processing that creates new experience." Both hypotheses were supported.

912. White, R. W. et al (1973). The concept of healthy personality: What do we really mean? Counseling Psychologist, 4(2), 3-68.

Provides the reader with a lead article by Robert White critical of the term self-actualization and offering an overview of the usefulness of the concept of healthy personality. Also included in this journal are articles by the following as they appear in the journal:

Cattell, R. B. The measurement of the healthy personality and the healthy society, 13-18.

Farnsworth, D. L. Comments on White's paper, 19-21.

Mowrer, O. H. Commendation and a few questions, 21-22.

Ansbacher, R. R. Comment of White's paper, 23-24.

DuBois, C. Comment of White's paper, 24-25.

Maddi, S. R. Ethics and psychotherapy: Remarks stimulated by White's paper, 26-29.

Shostrom, E. L. Self-actualization: A scientific ethic, 29-35.

Offer, D. A psychiatrist examines the concept of normality, 35-38.

Bardon, J. I. Reactions to White's disabuse of the concept of healthy personality, 38-41.

Shainess, N. Discussion of White's paper, 41-44.

Ellis, A. Can there be a rational concept of healthy personality, 45-47.

Smith, M. B. Comment on White's paper, 48-51.

Thoresen, C. E. The healthy personality as a sick trait, 51-56.

Heath, R. Form, flow and full-being: Response to White's paper, 56-63.

Goodstein, L. D. The place of values in the world of counseling, 63-66.

Patterson, C. H. Competence is not enough, 66-67.

White, R. W. What do I really mean? 67-68.

913. Wills, B. S. (1974). Personality variables which discriminate between groups differing in level of self-actualization. Journal of Counseling Psychology, 21(3), 222-227.

Sought to determine the relationship between self-actualization, self-concept, values and achievement motivation comparing a male and female population. The population was divided into 3 levels. Males and females differed in their level of self-actualization and different combinations of personality variables discriminated between them.

914. Wright, L. (1971, April). Components of positive mental health. _Journal of Consulting and Clinical Psychology, 36_(2), 277-280.

Investigated the 6 areas of mental health proposed by Jahoda through a 30-item inventory. The factor analyzed results revealed that Jahoda's 6 categories were collapsed into 4 and 2 additional factors were added. The author concludes that Jahoda's categories are incomplete.

Dissertations and Theses

915. Barfield, R. S. (1968). The realization of the self: A comparison of self-actualization in the writings of Carl Jung and Carl Rogers. _DAI, 29_(7), 2088A.

916. Baron, M. P. (1978) The cumulative and immediate effects of unstructured (journal) and structured (bipolar checklist) self-evaluative writing upon self-evaluation and self-actualization of male and female college students. _DAI, 39_(4), 1930B.

917. Bollendorf, R. F. (1976). Effects of isolation on anxiety, and on the use of social roles by volunteer subjects of varying degrees of self-actualization and identification with their environment. _DAI, 37_(8). 4854A.

918. Byrd, R. E. (1970). Self-actualization through creative risk taking: A new laboratory model. _DAI, 31_(12), 6712A.

919. Charnov, B. H. (1976). An investigation of the effect of military enculturation process on self-actualization and self-concept. _DAI, 36_(10, 5340B.

920. Checkon Jr., S. (1973). A study of the effect of moderator variables on the relationship between self-actualization and achievement. DAI, 34(5), 2431A.

921. Chinisci, R. A. (1976). Self-actualization, ego strength, and need-achievement as dimensions of Friedman and Rosenman's A-B personality typology. DAI, 37(7), 3601B.

922. Crawford Jr., R. F. (1979). The relationship of self-actualization and jury bias. DAI, 40(3), 1419B.

923. Davis, C. K. (1974). The implications of language for facilitating self-actualization. DAI, 35(12), 7523A.

924. Denniston, B. A. (1975). An experiment on the effect of various training models on growth toward self-actualization. DAI, 36(8), 5038A.

925. Edalatian, Z. M. N. (1984). Maturity as a cross-cultural construct: Concepts of Shams, Maslow, and Loevinger. DAI, 46(3), 978B.

926. Engeran, E. A. (1978). Self-actualization and the acquisition of communication and discrimination skills. DAI, 39(9), 5323A.

927. Frick, W. B. (1969). A holistic theory of healthy personality. DAI, 31(5), 2982B.

928. Gallop, M. K. (1981). Maslow and the Tarot: Self-actualization in theory and practice. DAI, 42(2), 745B.

929. Hightower, E. (1980). Self-actualization: Its problematical aspects. DAI, 41(9), 3558B.

930. Kalas, J. T. (1978). The relationship between self-actualization and psychological type. DAI, 40(2), 921B.

Self-Actualization

931. Kaufman, C. C. (1974). Nadir experiences and their after effects as related to age and self-actualization. DAI, 35(8), 4180B.

932. Keogh, A. (1978). Authenticity and self-actualization: A rapprochement between the philosophy of Heidegger and the psychology of Maslow. DAI, 39(7), 4323A.

933. Loeb, L. S. (1974). Failure to find a relationship between self-actualization, internal-external locus-of-control, and repression-sensitization, with field-independence. DAI, 35(7), 3558B.

934. Long, J. A. (1968). Self-actualization in a sample of high school boys: A test of some propositions from self-identity theory. DAI, 29(8), 2804A.

935. Mandt III, A. J. (1978). The metaphysics of activity: An inquiry into the self-actualization of an idea. DAI, 39(6), 3634A.

936. Margulis, M. (1971). Perceptual and cognitive correlates of self-actualization. DAI, 32(10), 6055B.

937. Martin, D. J. (1974). The influence of reference group interactions and differential treatment on measures of locus-of-control and self-actualization in teaching undergraduates. Unpublished doctoral dissertation, University of California, Berkeley.

938. McFarland, J. C. (1973). Dialogical communication and its relationship to self-actualization. DAI, 34(10), 6784A.

939. McFarlane, E. A. (1980). Effects of a cardiac rehabilitation program on the self-concept, self-actualization, and adjustment to illness of post-myocardial infarction males. DAI, 41(2), 522B.

940. Meikle, D. T. (1982). Formal operations, ego defenses, and mature personality development. DAI, 43(4), 1238B.

941. Michalowski, B. K. M. (1977). A test of Maslow's hypothesis regarding self-actualization level and philosophical humor preference. DAI, 39(11), 5570B.

942. Moriarty, A. R. (1976). Time perspective and the fully functioning person: A preliminary investigation. DAI, 37(5), 2749A.

943. Muller, M. J. (1981). Conflict-reporting in social desirability contests: Change in level of experiencing as a function of a social learning treatment, ego resilience, and self-actualization. DAI, 42(3), 1185B.

944. Newman, M. (1956). Personality differences between volunteers and non-volunteers for psychological investigations: Self-actualization of volunteers and non-volunteers for researches in personality and perception. DAI, 17(3), 684.

945. Offenstein, R. E. (1973). Self-actualization: A construct validation study. DAI, 33(5), 2379B.

946. Pasnak, M. F. D. (1968). Fashion innovators compared with non-innovators on clothing attitudes, self-actualization, and tolerance of ambiguity. DAI, 29(5), 1864B.

947. Peoples, K. M. (1981). The presence of social interest and autonomy as complementary features of genuine self-actualization in participants of the human potential movement. DAI, 42(5), 2076B.

948. Petosa, R. A. (1980). The relationship between stressful life events and self-actualization. DAI, 41(6), 2118B.

Self-Actualization

949. Phoenix, J. R. (1981). Positive and negative masculinity and femininity: Relationship to self-actualization, attitudes about change as rated by self and close others. DAI, 42(11), 4587B.

950. Poelling, R. K. (1971). A developmental study of Abraham H. Maslow's self-actualization theory. DAI, 33(2), 623A.

951. Rader, T. F. (1982). Facilitating self actualization through verbal self expression: A theoretical perspective. DAI, 43(4), 1029A.

952. Rawles, B. A. (1980). The influence of a mentor on the level of self-actualization of American scientists. DAI, 41(4), 1348A.

953. Richardson, R. L. (1979). Rural and urban differences in self-actualization, time competency, and locus of control. DAI, 41(1), 366B.

954. Rogers, M. I. (1968). Self-actualization as process. DAI, 39(9), 4380B.

955. Russell, J. K. (1974). A study of the relationships between self-actualization, self-concept and self-disclosure. DAI, 35(3), 1395B.

956. Sargent, A. A. H. (1980). A study of the relationship between self-actualization and role conflict-ambiguity among registered nurses. DAI, 41(12), 4460B.

957. Saussy, C. (1977). A study of the adequacy of Abraham Maslow's concept of the self to his theory of self-actualization. DAI, 38(11), 5548B.

958. Schenberg, R. G. (1973). The relation of time perspective and self-actualization to ego development. DAI, 34(9), 4641B.

959. Secor, J. (1973). Anxiety and self-actualization demonstrated by acute-care nurses and non-acute-care nurses. DAI, 35(2), 791A.

960. Seipp, K. M. (1983). Psychosocial maturity: A necessary prerequisite for self-actualization. DAI, 44(1), 327B.

961. Shafer, M. G. (1982). Self-actualization, mysticism, and psychic experience. DAI, 43(2), 513B.

962. Sherwood Jr., J. J. (1963). Self-identity and self-actualization: A theory and research. DAI, 24(3), 1273.

963. Sjostrom, D. E. (1977). The relationship between Jung's theory of psychological type and Maslow's theory of self-actualization. DAI, 39(11), 5589B.

964. Skomra, A. N. (1975). Abraham Maslow's self-actualization: A basis for using humanistic psychology in literary analysis. DAI, 36(11), 7372A.

965. Sobol, E. G. (1977). The relation between self-actualization and the baccalaureate nursing student's response to stress as evidenced by level of state-trait anxiety. DAI, 38(4), 1654B.

966. Stein, S. R. (1978). An investigation of the relationship between gender appropriate vocational interests, self-actualization, dogmatism, and Holland's six personal orientations. DAI, 39(3), 1350A.

967. Szura, J. P. (1973). The effects of defensiveness self-actualization and locus-of-control on a Herzberg replication. DAI, 34(6), 2991B.

968. Trenberth, G. I. (1976). Self-actualization and agential-intellectual/communion-intuitive aspects of human behavior. DAI, 37(9). 4709B.

969. Tsantilis, P. (1978). Self-actualization and degree of susceptibility to labeling effects. DAI, 39(7), 3543B.

970. Tyska, C. A. (1980). A comparative case study of self-actualization: Eleanor Roosevelt and Antoine d Saint-Exupery. Unpublished master's thesis, University of Illinois, Urbana-Champaign.

971. Wallhermfechtel, J. H. (1976). The relationship of social intelligence to self-actualization. DAI, 37(5), 2532B.

972. Waser, C. J. (1975). An examination of self-actualization and its relationship to time estimation and temporal experience. DAI, 36(12), 6404B.

973. Wathney, S. E. (1978). Effects of sensory isolation on self-actualization. DAI, 39(5), 2531B.

974. Wexler, D. A. (1972). Style and meaning in emotional experience: An exploratory study on the nature of self-actualization. Unpublished doctoral dissertation, University of Chicago, Chicago, Illinois.

975. White, H. M. (1970). An investigation of some characteristics of high and low self-actualization and their relationship to alienation from self and society. DAI, 31(10), 5142A.

976. Wills, B. S. (1972). The identification of variables discriminating between groups differing in level of self-actualization through the use of multiple discriminant analysis. DAI, 33(5), 2059A.

977. Wiseman, N. L. (1972). Identity of human figure drawings as a function of the age, sex, functional intelligence and self-actualization of the artist. DAI, 33(5), 2363B.

978. Wolf, A. W. (1980). Self-actualization as cognitive style: A multivariate study. <u>DAI</u>, <u>41</u>(7), 2947A.

979. Zeedyk, R. J. (1980). Selectivity of self-disclosure and self-actualization in college students. <u>DAI</u>, <u>41</u>(10), 3907B.

Values represent one part of the make up of self-actualizing people. Several of the major theorists list as one of the characteristics of self-actualization a core of values that seem to be universal, transcendent of time and culture. This section contains works on values, moral development and their relationship to various populations and other research concerns. Included here, as well, are the theoretical papers linking biology as a basis for values for human beings.

980. Daniels, M. (1984, January). The relationship between moral development and self-actualization. *Journal of Moral Education*, 13(1), 25-30.

Reviews the conceptual and empirical evidence of a relationship between self-actualization and moral development. The author discusses the implications and interpretations of the relationship for the theory of self-actualization.

981. Fisher, G. (1973). Felons' conception of societal self-actualization values. *Corrective Psychiatry and Journal of Social Therapy*, 19(1), 3-5.

When asked to fake good on a measure of self-actualization to please a hypothetical parole board, felons typically scored lower than when they represented themselves. The author views this result as suggesting that felons see society as holding values which suppress individual growth, spontaneity, self-discovery in favor of passively conforming to the expectations of society.

982. Fisher, G. & Silverstein, A. B. (1969). Self-actualization values of felons. *Journal of Humanistic Psychology*, 9, 66-70.

Suggests that felons are able to change their scores on the POI according to instructions describing a particular population. When asked to simulate good, poor and themselves they give the higher scores as themselves, then as simulating good and, finally, as simulating poor adjustment. The authors suggest that felons view themselves as more self-actualizing than the normal population.

983. Gunter, L. M. (1969, January-February). The developing nursing student: Part I. a study of self-actualizing values. Nursing Research, 18, 60-64.

Compared nursing students with college freshmen and a self-actualizing sample. The results were mixed with the nursing students showing themselves both more self-actualizing than the college freshmen on some scales of the POI and less self-actualizing than the self-actualizing sample on some scales of the POI.

984. Kendler, H. H. (1980, November). Self-fulfillment: Psychological fact or moral prescription: Academic Psychology Bulletin, 2(3), 287-295.

Argues that "psychology is unable to offer an unqualified authority upon which to base an ethical system to govern human behavior. Psychologists, however, can discover the empirical consequences of different ethical beliefs and therefore provide information upon which to make moral choices."

985. Lucas, L. F. & Tsujimoto, R. N. (1978, December). Self-actualization and moral judgment. Psychological Reports, 43(3, Pt. 1). 838.

Studied the relationship of moral judgment to self-actualization and found only weak support for the hypothesized positive relationship between them.

986. Maslow, A. H. (1967). A theory of metamotivation: The biological rooting of the value-life. Journal of Humanistic Psychology, 7(2), 93-127.
Reprinted a number of times.

Offers 28 propositions describing and explaining the concept of metamotivation and the possibility of human biology as a source of life values.

987. Maslow, A. H. (1963). Fusions of facts and values. American Journal of Psychoanalysis, 23, 117-131. Reprinted in The Ethical Forum (1966), #5.

Presents a very thorough discussion of the problem of the place of values in scientific research. Maslow argues that science must not only consider values in its investigations but can also be considered a source of values since science can be used to discover values.

988. Maslow, A. H. (1954, March). Normality, health and values. Main Currents, 10(4), 75-81.

Discusses a re-definition of the word normality away from adjustment and toward self-actualization. Maslow argues that the systems of control and extreme environmentalism were changing (in 1954) and that the direction was toward what is presently labeled self-actualization.

Dissertations and Theses

989. Barton, A. (1965). Therapist values, self-actualization values, and other dimensions of the Q-sort in relation to therapeutic movement. Unpublished doctoral disseration, University of Chicago, Chicago, Illinois.

990. Damsbo, A. M. (1975). Self-actualization and value-enhancement employing hypnotic suggestion. DAI, 36(6), 2998B.

991. Goodman, R. M. (1980). The relationship between meaning in life and sense of belonging to self-actualization and open-mindedness among members of a value-based organization. DAI, 41(1), 165A.

992. Gruver, E. W. (1975). A study of the relationship between self-actualization and moral development. DAI, 36(3), 1407B.

993. Lindskoog, D. P. (1972). Some life history, attitudinal, and moral development correlates of self-actualization among evangelical seminary students. DAI, 33(9), 4492B.

994. McDonnell, P. A. (1979). Personal development of school administrators: Self-concept, self-actualization, moral judgment and ego development. DAI, 40(7), 3668A.

995. Moore, M. L. (1976). Effects of value clarification on dogmatism, critical thinking, and self-actualization. DAI, 37(2), 907A.

996. Ormond, H. A. (1973). Relationship of measurements of dogmatism, purpose in life, and self-actualization. DAI, 34(4), 1730B.

997. Rehberg, C. E. (1973). A comparison of values and behaviors in the development of self-actualization of values and behaviors in the development of youth corps enrollees in West Central Wisconsin. DAI, 34(11), 5661B.

998. Walker, N. P. (1968). Clothing expenditures as related to selected values, self-actualization, and buying practices: An exploratory study. DAI, 29(12), 4836B.

Self-Actualization

999. Weiss, J. (1980). Self-actualization and moral maturity: The relationship between degrees of self-actualization and levels of moral maturity in selected undergraduate college students. DAI, 40(9), 4974A.

This section concerns the relationship of self-actualization to a number of concerns in the Woman's Movement. It is an area that deserves more study and one that has been neglected. Research questions concern whether men and women have different patterns of self-actualization, whether the concept of self-actualization is value loaded in favor of men since so many of the theorists are men and the relationship of self-actualization to females choices regarding life-style (career vs. home, marriage vs. single living, children or not). Each of these area offers opportunities for students to investigate.

1000. Brashear, D. B. & Willis, K. (1976, July). Claiming our own: A model for women's growth. <u>Journal of Marriage and Family Counseling</u>, <u>2</u>(3), 251-258.

Develops what the authors label the "ownership model" as a "framework in which women can develop themselves, often without risk to marriage."

1001. Cristall, L. & Dean, R. S. (1976, December). Relationship of sex-role stereotypes and self-actualization. <u>Psychological Reports</u>, <u>39</u>(3, Pt. 1), 842.

Examined the differences in androgyny among adults with different levels of self-actualization. The results indicate no significant differences between males and females on either self-actualization or androgyny scores. Further, it appeared that high self-actualizers were also high in androgyny scores.

1002. Dietch, J. (1978, December). Love, Sex roles, and psychological health. <u>Journal of Personality Assessment</u>, <u>42</u>(6), 626-634.

Discovered that females have higher levels of B-love than males. Further, it was reported that person who had been in a love relationship were higher in self-actualization than persons who reported never being in love. Persons higher in self-actualization reported less resentment toward their ex-lover than did low scorers.

1003. Doyle, J. A. (1975, December). Self-actualization and attitudes toward women. Psychological Reports, 37(3, Pt. 1), 899-902.

Studied the relationship between self-actualization and feminist-antifeminist beliefs. The results show that there is a small positive relationship between high self-actualization scores and profeminist attitudes.

1004. Drews, E. M. (1965). Counseling for self-actualization in gifted girls and young women. Journal of Counseling Psychology, 12, 167-175.

Reports that even though intellectually gifted young women report higher growth motivation they are not able to act on their desires. The author discusses counseling approaches which will free the gifted toward self-actualization.

1005. Ginn, R. O. (1975, December). Psychological androgyny and self-actualization. Psychological Reports, 37(3, Pt. 1), 886.

Examined the relationship of androgyny to self-actualization. The Bem Sex-role Inventory divided subjects into masculine, androdynous and feminine categories. "Contrary to prediction androgynous subjects scored no differently on the measures of self-actualization than either masculine or feminine subjects."

1006. Hjelle,   L.   A.   (1975,   November).
Relationship of social interest to internal-
external control and   self-actualization   in
young   women.   Journal   of   Individual
Psychology, 31(2), 171-174.

Studied Adler's concept of Social   Interest,
self-actualization   and   locus   of   control.
Social   Interest   had   a   high,   positive
correlation   with   both   internal   locus   of
control and self-actualization.

1007. Hjelle, L. A. & Butterfield, R.   (1974,
July).   Self-actualization   and   women's
attitudes   toward   their   roles in contemporary
society. Journal of Psychology, 87(2), 225-
230.

Investigated   college   women's   attitudes
toward   women's rights and roles in society.
The   women   were   divided   into   groups   of
conservative   and   liberal   women.   "The
results indicated   substantial   support   for
the   prediction   that   women   professing
liberal,   profeminist   attitudes   are   more
self-actualized   than   women   endorsing
traditional social role attitudes."

1008. Humphrey, M. & Lenham C. (1984, September).
Adolescent fantasy and self-fulfillment: The
problem of female   passivity.   Journal   of
Adolescence, 7(3), 295-304.

Studied   differences   in   goals for boys and
girls, men and women   from   written   essays
remembering   the   day they left high school.
The major difference   had   to   do   with   the
degree   to   which   girls   were more oriented
toward marriage and family life,   boys   more
career   oriented and, in general, a tendency
for the girls "being ready to   live   through
others rather than on their own terms."

1009. King, M.   (1974, August). Sex differences
in   self-actualization.   Psychological
Reports, 35(1, Pt. 2), 602.

Reports   sex   differences   in   self-actualization for married couples. There were no significant differences in this study. The author suggests that this provides support for Maslow's contention that self-actualizing people choose other self-actualizers as mates.

1010. Loeffler, D. & Fielder, L. (1979, January). Woman - a sense of identity: A counseling intervention to facilitate personal growth in women. Journal of Counseling Psychology, 26(1), 51-57.

Designed, implemented and evaluated an intervention "with the goal of facilitating the psychological growth of women. Focus was on increased self-esteem and competence through self-awareness, skills development, cognitive changes, and changes in overt behavior." Reports 3 different studies of the intervention suggesting its effectiveness.

1011. McVicar, P. & Herman, A. (1983, April). Assertiveness, self-actualization and locus of control in women. Sex Roles, 9(4), 555-562.

Designed an intervention program to facilitate psychological growth in middle-aged women. Measures of self-actualization, assertiveness and locus of control were taken before and after the intervention. Clear changes in assertiveness and self-actualization were noted while no change in locus of control occurred during the intervention. The authors note that the women were characterized by an internal locus of control at the pre-test and remained so after the intervention which accounts for no change.

1012. Niesz, N. L. (1977, October). Periodicity and self-actualization in women. Journal of Clinical Psychology. 33(4), 1014-1017.

Studied the relationship between menstrual cycle and a measure of self-

actualization. Three groups were
identified: premenstrual, menstrual and
midcycle. The results indicate that the
menstrual group's scores were significantly
higher on a measure of self-actualization
than the midcycle group. The difference
between the premenstrual and menstrual group
was in the same direction but not
significant.

1013. Olczak, P. V. & Goldman, J. A. (1981,
June). Relationship between self-
actualization and assertiveness in males and
females. Psychological Reports, 48(3), 931-
937.

Related self-actualization and
assertiveness. The results show differences
between males and females were
nonsignificant. The relationship between
high self-actualization and assertiveness
was moderately high.

1014. Podeschi, R. L. & Podeschi, P. J. (1973-
1974, Winter). Abraham Maslow: On the
potential of women. Educational Horizons,
52(2), 61-64.

Presents the authors' views of the
contributions of Maslow's work for the
development of women.

1015. Priest, R. F. & Wilhelm, P. G. (1974,
April). Sex, marital status, and
self/actualization as factors in the
appreciation of sexist jokes. Journal of
Social Psychology, 92(2), 245-249.

Studied self-actualization and appreciation
of sexist humor. The outcome was that self-
actualizers tended to prefer profemale jokes
but Maslow's concept that self-actualizers
would find sex-conflict humor distasteful
was not supported.

1016. Schroeder, C. C. (1973). Sex differences and growth toward self-actualization during the freshman year. Psychological Reports, 32(2), 416-418.

Investigated scores of college freshmen for differences between males and females. Such differences were found and the author recommends that scores from male and female populations not be pooled.

1017. Symonds, A. (1980, Winter). The stress of self-realization. American Journal of Psychoanalysis, 40(4), 293-300.

Reports the development of Karen Horney's theories of self-realization and provides a historical background for its development.

1018. Valle, V. A. & Koeske, G. F. (1974). Sex differences in the relationship of POI self-actualization to other adjustment and maturity measures. Personality and Social Psychology Bulletin, 1(1), 310-312.

Investigated the relationship between self-actualization, moral reasoning and locus of control. The results were that self-actualization was significantly related to internal locus of control and slightly to moral reasoning only for males.

1019. Vander Wilt, R. B. & Klocke, R. A. (1971, Spring). Self-actualization of females in an experimental orientation program. Journal of the National Association of Women Deans and Counselors, 34(3), 125-129.

Reports on an outward bound orientation for college students that had a significant effect on entering female freshman students.

1020. Wassell, B. B. (1980, Winter). New frontiers in Horney theory of self-realization. American Journal of Psychoanalysis, 40(4), 333-346.

Provides historical background and

227

emphasizes the development of Horney's ideas toward self-realization as a biological, evolutionary force in all persons.

Dissertations and Theses

1021. Aguren, C. T. (1974). An exploration of self-actualization, self-concept, locus of control, and other characteristics as exhibited in selected mature community college women. DAI, 35(12), 7641A.

1022. Beach, B. J. (1980). Lesbian and nonlesbian women: Profiles of development and self-actualization. DAI, 42(3), 1199B.

1023. Blacher, J. (1977). An exploration of androgyny, self-actualization, and field-independence in lesbian feminist and non-feminist and non-lesbian feminist and non-feminist women. DAI, 39(9), 4568B.

1024. Bottoms, L. W. (1982). The interrelationships among sex-role orientation, self-actualization, and significant issues of high-achieving, executive women. DAI, 43(6), 2027B.

1025. Brennan, L. M. (1973). The correlation of self-actualization, selected background variables and involvement in social organizations and activities of women in three national Catholic organizations. DAI, 34(8), 4728A.

1026. Brooks, A. M. T. (1978). An analysis of female self-concept, self-actualization, and power-related personality factors as dimensions of power in female nurses with earned doctoral degrees. DAI, 39(3), 1208B.

1027. Burr, R. L. (1974). The effects of same-sex and mixed-sex growth groups on measures of self-actualization and verbal behavior of females. DAI, 35(11), 7117A.

Self-Actualization

1028. Clarke, P. N. (1983). Body weight: Perceived effect on life, conversational distance, and self-actualization. DAI, 44(12), 3717B.

1029. Collins Jr., E. L. (1979). Sex-role perceptions and self-actualization among high school female athletes and nonathletes. DAI, 41(1), 160A.

1030. Cristall, L. M. (1978). A comparison of androgyny and self-actualization in battered women. DAI, 39(10), 5039B.

1031. Cust, M. A. (1978). Self-actualization and psychological androgyny in a sample of university women. Unpublished doctoral dissertation, University of Alberta, Canada.

1032. Danielson, D. W. (1980). The relationship between perceived self-actualization, perceived orgastic frequency, and sexual knowledge in women. DAI, 41(12), 4636B.

1033. Darpli, F. (1974). The relationship of involvement in the womens' liberation movement and measured self-actualization. DAI, 35(3), 1378B.

1034. Dries, R. M. (1975). The divorced woman: Measurement of self-actualization change and self-concept. DAI, 36(2), 884B.

1035. Dugan, S. M. (1981). The relationship of personality to emotional fluctuations associated with the menstrual cycle. DAI, 42(9), 3863B.

1036. Erb, M. E. (1976). Toward women's fuller humanness: Self-actualization of women as related to sex-role values, psychological qualities and relationships. DAI, 38(9), 4451B.

1037. Ferrier, M. J. (1973). Self-actualization and achievement motivation in college women. DAI, 34(8), 4737A.

Self-Actualization

1038. Fitzpatrick, G. (1982). Self-disclosure of lesbianism as related to self-actualization and self-stigmatization. DAI, 43(12), 4143.

1039. Fonte, V. H. (1976). Demographic variables and self-actualization for divorced and married women. DAI, 38(9), 4452B.

1040. Ford, D. S. (1981). The relationship between multidimensional locus of control, sex role, self actualization, and feminist/traditional attitudes toward women. DAI, 42(5), 2055B.

1041. Gamble, D. H. (1981). The effects of group counseling vs self-directed reading on androgyny, self-actualization and academic achievement of college females of varying academic ability. DAI, 42(8), 3399B.

1042. Gill, M. K. (1974). Psychological femininity of college women as it relates to self-actualization, feminine role attitudes, and selected background variables. DAI, 36(11), 7206A.

1043. Glass, C. A. (1981). The differences of individuals with type A and type B behavior patterns and the women's awareness seminar on self-actualization and flexibility. DAI, 42(10), 4363A.

1044. Hamm, B. C. (1967). A study of the differences between self-actualization scores and product perceptions among female consumers. DAI, 27(12), 4007A.

1045. Harder, J. M. (1969). Self-actualization, mood, and personality adjustment in married women. DAI, 31(2), 897B.

1046. Harris, L. S. (1977). The relation of androgyny to self-actualization, locus of control, and differential regard for the sexes. DAI, 38(2), 899B.

Self-Actualization

1047. Hart, S. J. (1979). The effects of student centered orientation groups on situation-specific anxiety, self-actualization, and adjustment to school, in high school freshman females. DAI, 39(11), 6653A.

1048. Heideman, G. A. (1976). Effects of traditional versus non-traditional sex-role orientation on personality androgyny and self-actualization. DAI, 38(3), 1468B.

1049. Henderson, J. M. (1975). The effects of assertiveness training on self-actualization in women. DAI, 36(7), 3575B.

1050. Hunt, P. L. (1975). Female child care workers: Their feminine identity congruence, attitudes toward women, self-actualization and marital status. DAI, 36(7), 4262A.

1051. Johnston, A. D. (1981). Sex role and self-actualization in women over 30 years of age. DAI, 42(2), 748B.

1052. Katz, E. A. (1976). The belief in androgyny and the development of self-actualization. DAI, 36(11), 7129A.

1053. Kowalski, J. (1984). The relationship between self-actualization and participation in congregation-sponsored growth programs for women within the Adrian Dominican congregation. DAI, 45(6), 1953B.

1054. Lee, H. N. (1978). The difference between self-actualization and marital adjustment of females whose formal education terminated at the high school and college levels. DAI, 39(12), 7136A.

1055. Lippert, J. G. (1975). Parental child-rearing attitudes and behaviors as antecedents of self-actualization in females. DAI, 36(12), 6388B.

1056. Manning, T. T. (1973). Career motivation, ego development and self-actualization in adult women. DAI, 34(11), 5657B.

1057. Martin, R. P. T. (1981). Self-disclosure of successful women administrators in Las Vegas, Nevada. DAI, 42(2), 833B.

1058. Matthews, L. J. (1979). Comparisons of self-actualization among three groups of college women. DAI, 40(1), 154A.

1059. Mayfield, D. M. (1981). An investigation of the effects of a ten-week aerobic dance program on cardiorespiratory functioning, body composition and self-actualization of selected females. DAI, 42(10), 4352A.

1060. McKinley, M. C. (1978). The effect of a psychology of personal growth course on levels of self-actualization and psychological androgyny in mature women students. DAI, 39(3), 1346A.

1061. McKissick, G. C. (1975). The relationship among the factors of academic ability, self-actualization, and achievement of seniors in a four-year liberal arts college for women. DAI, 37(4), 2016A.

1062. Milton, D. A. (1983). The relationship between cognitive style, self-actualization, and trait anxiety in young adult women. DAI, 44(7), 2096.

1063. Murphy, J. P. (1984). Guilt and self-actualization in the professionally employed mother. DAI, 45(10), 3342B.

1064. Ohlbaum, J. S. (1971). Self-concepts, value characteristics and self-actualization of professional and non-professional women. DAI, 32(2), 1221B.

1065. Ott, T. J. (1976). Androgyny, sex roles stereotypes, sex role attitudes and self-actualization among college women. DAI, 37(6), 3527A.

Self-Actualization

1066. Poole, R. J. (1977). A comparative study of the effects of assertive training and career decision-making counseling on self-concept, self-actualization and feelings of inadequacy of adult women community college students. DAI, 38(4), 1902A.

1067. Potash, M. S. (1978). Androgyny and its relation to behavioral rigidity and self-actualization in women college students. DAI, 38(12), 6124B.

1068. Ritter, M. I. H. (1981). The minister's wife: An exploratory study on role conflict and self actualization. DAI, 43(4), 1265B.

1069. Rohaly, K. A. (1971). The relationship between movement participation, movement satisfaction, self-actualization, and trait anxiety in selected college freshmen women. DAI, 32(7), 3766A.

1070. Schmalz, M. B. (1983). Self-actualization in women and its relationship to motherhood, educational background, employment status, and present age. DAI, 45(9), 3010A.

1071. Smith, H. R. (1978). The relationship between androgyny and self-actualization in college men and women. DAI, 39(11), 6662A.

1072. Snyder, J. J. (1978). Factors relating to self-actualization and motivation to achieve in learning among college women. DAI, 38(12), 7244A.

1073. Vigilanti, M. A. (1980). The effects of sex-role attitudes on womens' self-actualization and life satisfaction. DAI, 41(5), 1983B.

1074. Weissman, E. I. (1974). The relationship between the marital status, feminine identity conflict, and self-actualization of women doctoral students. DAI, 35(6), 3441A.

1075. Williams, L. J. (1980). A comparative study of self-actualization of female alcoholics in Alcoholics Anonymous. DAI, 41(1), 337B.

1076. Wimberly, C. E. (1979). Self actualization and the minister's wife. DAI, 41(11), 4280B.

1077. Wisch, P. B. (1976). A profile of mature returning women at Temple University in September, 1974 and the effects of a special seminar on their levels of anxiety and potential for self-actualization during their first semester. DAI, 37(1), 209A.

1078. Wysocki, S. R. (1975). Differential effects of three group treatments on self-actualization and attitudes toward the sex roles of women. DAI, 36(11), 7316A.

1079. Ziegler, S. M. (1977). Androgyny in nursing: Nurse role expectation, satisfaction, academic achievement, and self-actualization in male and female students. DAI, 38(5), 2124B.

Self-Actualization

Books

The books in this section represent the major works of the major theorists as well as books that probably fall into the category of "self-help" books that in and of themselves do not contribute much to the overall theory of self-actualization. The editors have not sought to edit out any book that in our knowledge dealt with the topic of self-actualization. These works constitute the most important writing done on self-actualization and, we believe, represent most of the book length works done on self-actualization in the English language.

1080. Academy of Religion and Mental Health. (1959). Religion, science, and mental health: Proceedings of the first academy symposium on inter-discipline responsibility for mental health - a religious and scientific concern - 1957. New York: New York University Press.

1081. Allport, G. (1968). The person in psychology. Boston: Beacon Press.

1082. Allport, G. (1961). Pattern and growth in personality. New York: Holt, Rinehart and Winston.

1083. Allport, G. (1960). Personality and social encounter. Boston: Beacon Press..

1084. Allport, G. (1955). Becoming. New Haven, Connecticut: Yale University Press.

1085. Barron, F. (1963). Creativity and psychological health. New York: Van Nostrand Reinhold.

1086. Bertocci, P. & Millard, R. (1963). Personality and the good. New York: McKay.

1087. Buber, M. (1970). I and thou. New York: Charles Scribners and Sons.

1088. Bugenthal, J. (Ed.). Challenges of humanistic psychology. New York: McGraw-Hill.

1089. Buhler, C. (1971). The way to fulfillment: Psychological techniques (translated by D. J. Baker). New York: Hawthorn.

1090. Buhler, C. & Massarik, F. (Eds.). (1968). The course of human life: A study of life goals in the humansitic perspective. New York: Springer.

1091. Carkhuff, R. R. (1981). Toward actualizing human potential. Amherst, Massachusetts: Human Resource Development Press.

1092. Chiang, H. & Maslow, A. H. (1977). The healthy personality: Readings (2nd. Ed.). New York: D. Van Nostrand.

1093. Coan, R. W. (1977). Hero, artist, sage or saint?: A survey of views on what is variously called mental health, normality, maturity, self-actualization, and human fulfillment. New York: Columbia University Press.

1094. Combs, A. W., Richards, A. C. & Richards, F. (1976). Perceptual psychology: A humanistic approach to the study of persons. (3rd Ed.). New York: Harper and Row.

1095. Combs, A. W. (Ed.). (1962). Perceiving, behaving, becoming: A new focus on education. Washington, D. C.: Association for Supervision and Curriculum Development.

1096. Combs, A. W. (Ed.). (1961). Personality theory and counseling practice. Gainesville, Florida: University of Florida Press.

Self-Actualization

1097. Crumbaugh, J. C. (1973). Everything to gain: A guide to self-fulfillment through logoanalysis. Chicago, Illinois: Nelson-Hall.

1098. Emery, S. & Rogin, N. (1978). Actualizations: You don't have to rehearse to be yourself. Garden City, New York: Doubleday.

1099. English, H. & English A. (Eds.). (1958). Self-actualization: A comprehensive dictionary of psychological and psychoanalytic terms. New York: Longmans, Green.

1100. Evans, R. I. (Ed.). (1975). Carl Rogers: The man and his ideas. New York: E. P. Dutton.

1101. Fitts, W. H. et al (1971). The self-concept and self-actualization. Nashville, Tennessee: Dede Wallace Center.

1102. Frankl, V. (1975). The unconscious god. New York: Simon and Schuster.

1103. Frankl, V. (1969). The will to meaning. Cleveland, Ohio: World Publishing.

1104. Frankl, V. (1965). The doctor and the soul (2nd. Ed.). New York: Knofp.

1105. Frankl, V. (1962). Man's search for meaning. Boston: Beacon Press.

1106. Freedman, J. L. (1978). Happy people: What happiness is, who has it, and why. New York: Harcourt, Brace and Jovanovich.

1107. Fromm, E. (1968). The revolution of hope. New York: Harper and Row.

1108. Fromm, E. (1955). The sane society. New York: Holt, Rinehart and Winston.

1109. Fromm, E. (1947). Man for himself. New York: Holt, Rinehart and Winston.

1110. Fromm, E. (1941). Escape from freedom. New York: Holt, Rinehart and Winston.

1111. Goble, F. G. (1970). The third force: The psychology of Abraham Maslow. New York: Pocket Books.

1112. Hooker, D. (1977). The healthy personality and the Christian life. North Quincy, Massachusetts: Chistopher Publishing House.

1113. Jahoda, M. (1958). Current concepts of positive mental health. New York: Basic Books.

1114. Jourard, S. M. (1971). The transparent self. New York: Van Nostrand Reinhold Company.

1115. Jourard, S. M. (1968). Disclosing man to himself. New York: Van Nostrand Reinhold Company.

1116. Jourard, S. M. (Ed.). To be or not to be...: Existential-psychological perspectives on the self. Gainesville, Florida: University of Florida Press.

1117. Jourard, S. M. & Landsman, T. (1980). Healthy Personality: An approach from the viewpoint of humanistic psychology. (4th Ed.). New York: MacMillan Publishing Company.

1118. Jung, C. G. (1968). Man and his symbols. New York: Dell Publishing.

1119. Jung, C. G. (1961). Memories, dreams, reflections. New York: Vantage Books.

1120. Jung, C. G. (1954). The development of personality. New York: Pantheon.

1121. Jung, C. G. (1953). Two essays on analytical psychology. New York: Pantheon.

1122. Jung, C. G. (1933). Modern man in search of a soul. New York: Harcourt, Brace.

Self-Actualization

1123. Knapp, R. R. (1976). Handbook for the Personal Orientation Inventory. San Diego, California: Educational and Industrial Testing Service.

1124. Knapp, R. R. (1971). The measurement of self-actualization and its theoretical implications. San Diego, California: Educational and Industrial Testing Service.

1125. Laski, M. (1961). Ecstacy: A study of some secular and religious experiences. London: Cresset Press.

1126. Lowry, R. J. (1973). A. H. Maslow: An intellectual portrait. Monterey, California: Brooks/Cole Publishing Company.

1127. Lowry, R. J. (Ed.). Dominance, self-esteem, self-actualization: Germinal papers of A. H. Maslow. Monterey, California: Brooks/Cole Publishing Company.

1128. Lowry, R. J. (Ed.). The journals of A. H. Maslow, volumes I and II. Monterey, California: Brooks/Cole Publishing Company.

1129. Maslow, A. H. (1971). Farther reaches of human nature. New York: Viking Press.

1130. Maslow, A. H. (1970). Motivation and personality. (2nd Ed.). New York: Harper and Row.

1131. Maslow, A. H. (1968). Toward a psychology of being. New York: Van Nostrand Company.

1132. Maslow, A. H. (1966). The psychology of science: A reconnaissance. New York: Harper and Row. Paperback edition (1969). Chicago, Illinois: Henry Regnery Company.

1133. Maslow, A. H. (1965). Eupsychian management: A journal. Homewood, Illinois: Richard D. Irwin, Inc. and The Dorsey Press.

1134. Maslow, A. H. (1964). Religions, values and peak experiences. New York: Viking Press.

1135. Maslow, B. G. (Compiled with the assistance of). (1972). Abraham H. Maslow: A memorial volume. Monterey, California: Brooks/Cole Publishing Company.

1136. Moustakas, C. (Ed.). (1956). The self. New York: Harper and Row.

1137. Murphy, M. (1978). The psychic side of sports. Reading, Massachusetts: Addison-Wesley.

1138. Perls, F. (1973). The gestalt approach. Ben Lomond: California: Science and Behavior Books.

1139. Perls, F. (1972). In and out of the garbage pail. New York: Bantam Books. Also (1969) Lafayette, California: Real People Press.

1140. Perls, F. (1969). Gestalt therapy verbatim. Lafayette, California: Real People Press.

1141. Perls. F. (1947). Ego, hunger, and aggression. New York: Random House.

1142. Rogers, C. R. (1980). A way of being. Boston, Massachusetts: Houghlin-Mifflin Company.

1143. Rogers, C. R. (1961). On becoming a person. Boston, Massachusetts: Houghlin-Mifflin Company.

1144. Samples, B. & Wohlford, B. (1973). Opening: A primer for self-actualization. Menlo Park, California: Addison-Wesley.

Self-Actualization

1145. Schafer, R. C. (1977). The magic of self-actualization: The development of human potential from where you are, to where you want to be. Des Moines, Iowa: Behavioral Research Foundation.

1146. Schultz, D. (1977). Growth psychology: Models of the healthy personality. New York: Van Nostrand.

1147. Seeman, J. (1983). Personality integration: Studies and reflections. New York: Human Sciences Press.

1148. Severin, F. (Ed.). (1965). Humanistic viewpoints in psychology. New York: McGraw-Hill.

1149. Shostrom E. L. (with L. Knapp and R. R. Knapp). (1976). Actualizing therapy: Foundations for a scientific ethic. San Diego, California: EdITS Publishers.

1150. Shostrom, E. L. (1974). Personal orientation dimensions. San Diego, California: Educational and Industrial Testing Service.

1151. Shostrom, E. L. (1972). Freedom to be. Englewood Cliffs, New Jersey: Prentice-Hall. Paperback edition (1973). New York: Bantam Books.

1152. Shostrom, E. L. (1968). Bibliography for the P. O. I. San Diego, California: Educational and Industrial Testing Service.

1153. Shostrom, E. L. (1967). Man, the manipulator. Nashville, Tennessee: Abingdon Press. Paperback edition (1968). New York: Bantam Books.

1154. Shostrom, E. L. (1963). Personal orientation inventory (POI): A test of self-actualization. San Diego, California: Educational and Industrial Testing Service.

1155. Sutich, A. & Vich, M. (1969). Readings in humanistic psychology. New York: Free Press.

1156. Tillich, P. (1952). The courage to be. New Haven, Connecticut: Yale University Press.

1157. Trueblood, R. W. & McHolland, J. D. (1979). Self-actualization and the human potential group process. Evanston, Illinois: Kendall College.

1158. Valett, R. (1974). Self-actualization. Niles, Illinois: Argus Communications.

Author Index

Author Index

Author Index

Green, E. J., 182
Greentree III, I. S., 781
Greer, J. F., 183
Gregory Jr., J. F., 314
Griesman, R., 637
Griggs, M. B., 89
Grinker, R. A., 824
Grisham, J. H., 638
Groeneveld, L. C., 639
Grossack, M. M., 825
Grossman, B. B., 184
Groves, D. L., 826
Gruenbaum, M., 770
Gruver, E. W., 992
Gundersheim, J., 773, 782
Gunn, B. 358
Gunn, S. H., 774
Gunnison, H., 539
Gunter, L. M., 983

Hageseth, J. A., 827
Hall, D. T., 432
Hall, J. C., 640
Hamm, B. C., 433, 1044
Hammond, S., 14
Hamon, S. A., 736
Hampden-Turner, C. 42
Hampton, J. D., 90
Hancock, P., 359
Hannigan, P. S., 546,
 557, 558, 641
Hanson, J. J., 642
Hardeman, M., 828
Harder, J. M., 1045
Hargadine, M. P., 783
Harper, F. B., 480, 481,
 489
Harris, L. 332
Harris, L. S., 1046
Hartlieb, C. J., 185
Hart, S. J., 1047
Hartnett, J., 839
Hartsell, J. E., 186
Hattie, J., 359
Hawkins, H. H., 187
Hawkins, M., 480
Hayakawa, S. I., 829

Hayes III, P. L., 643
Heath, R., 912
Heggoy, S. J., 188
Heideman, G. A., 1048
Heintschel, R. M., 189
Hekmat, H., 561
Helms, J. E., 484
Henderson, D. B., 190
Henderson, J. M., 1049
Henjum, A., 91
Hensley, J. H., 360
Herman, A., 1011
Hersch, L. E., 315
Hershenson, D. B., 562
Hightower, E., 929
Hill, C. E., 593
Hines, C. C. W., 191
Hines, R. F., 644
Hirsh, E., 377
Hix, J. A., 360
Hjelle, L. A., 287, 459
 513, 737, 830, 1006,
 1007
Hoffman, M. B., 479
Hoffman, S., 403
Hogan, H. W., 831
Hogan, W. J., 192
Holt, D. D., 193
Honigman, I., 377
Hood Jr., R. W., 738
Hood, W. D., 645
Hooker, D., 1112
Hoover, E. A., 758
Horowitz, R. S., 646
Horton, R. E., 21
Hounshell, P. B., 69
Hoy, W. K., 73
Huber, R. J., 832
Hull, D., 647
Hull, J. A., 194
Hulsey, C. L., 195
Hummel, J. F., 6
Humphrey, M., 1008
Hungerman, P. W., 648
Hunt, D. L., 1050
Huntsman, K. H., 92
Husa, H. E., 93
Hyde, M. S., 538

247

Author Index

Author Index

Subject Index

Science, 115, 128, 146, 189, 248, 863, 1080
Scientists, 10, 128, 952
Self, 799, 962
Self-becoming, 802
Self-concept, 191, 192, 491, 492, 630, 683, 705, 709, 714, 724, 727, 729, 839, 955, 994, 1026, 1034, 1064, 1066, 1100
Self-disclosure, 313, 573, 623, 731, 753, 834, 837, 955, 979, 1057
Self-esteem, 224, 255, 319, 322, 465, 722, 1112
Self-fulfillment, 747, 797
Self-identity theory, 934
Self-realization, 1017
Self-transformation, 870
Seminary students, 743
Sensitivity training, 543, 544, 545, 559, 560, 571, 572, 583, 584, 585, 615, 705, 711, 718, 740, 759
Sensory isolation, 973
Sex, 728, 768, 769, 770
Sex differences, 1009, 1016
Sex role, 1028, 1036, 1048, 1051, 1073, 1078,
Sex role perception, 279, 321, 706, 792, 1001, 1002, 1024, 1065
Sexual activity, 5
Shams, 292
Single sex schools, 251
Sixteen Personal Factor Inventory, 411
Small business owners, 436, 448
Smuts, Jan, 795
Social intelligence, 971
Social interest, 1006
Social studies, 80, 172
Sociopathy, 502
Somatic complaints, 238

Special education, 271
Spinal cord injury, 298, 321, 326
Sports, 529, 771-793, 1121
Stephen the Martyr, 736
Stress, 948
Students, 73, 78, 82, 106, 109, 123, 132, 140, 141, 164, 176, 193, 194, 207, 221, 262, 937
Student personnel, 66
Student teachers, 137, 160, 173, 193
Substance abuse, 516, 650
Supervision, 444, 449, 546, 593
Supervisor, 438, 685
Survival training, 771

Tarot, 928
Teachers, 27, 28, 68, 69, 71, 75, 80, 81, 91, 96, 103, 107, 109, 112, 131, 132, 141, 143, 148, 149, 151, 163, 164, 183, 184, 194, 195, 198, 204, 218, 219, 221, 222, 224, 225, 230, 232, 241, 244, 258, 261, 268, 423
Teacher education, 94, 272, 273, 276
Teacher training, 157, 219
Teaching methods, 133
Technology, 124
Tennis, 772
T-group, 542, 576, 577, 730
Theological students, 759
Theory, 794-979
Tillich, Paul, 755

261

Reference Report Form

Dear Reader:

   If you know of a source or sources not
included in this book please send the information
to the address below. The new source will be
included in a future revision which will include
missing references as well as updating this volume
for future years.

   Please send any information to:

            Dr. David Welch
            Counseling Psychology
            University of Northern Colorado
            Greeley, Colorado 80631